An Easier Way

An Easier Way
Handbook for
the Elderly and
Handicapped

Jean Vieth Sargent

Artwork by Linda Emmerson,
Dana Thiermann, and
Sue Collins

Iowa State University Press
Ames, Iowa / 1 9 8 1

Jean Vieth Sargent's column, "An Easier Way," appears weekly in the *Ames Tribune* and *Cedar Rapids Gazette*. She received her B.S. and M.S. degrees from Iowa State University; her research concerned elderly arthritic homemakers. She has been a member of the Home Economics Department of the University of Utah, Director of an Adult Nutrition Activity Program in Salt Lake City, and her professional and volunteer work has focused primarily on the elderly and handicapped.

© 1981 The Iowa State University Press
All rights reserved. Composed and printed by The Iowa State University Press, Ames, Iowa 50010

First edition, 1981
International Standard Book Number: 0-8138-0870-7

Library of Congress Catalog Card Number: 81-81508

CONTENTS

FOREWORD

An Easier Way has been written to capture the attention of the millions of persons with physical disabilities who will benefit from the equipment and devices illustrated and described on the following pages. Jean Vieth Sargent has made a contribution to the handicapped and elderly by her suggestions and ideas for performing the work of the home and personal care.

For the 10 million persons with severe disabilities who wish to remain independent in personal care and housekeeping activities, these suggestions translate into a capability to live by themselves. Many others will discover here ways to reduce both the time and energy required for the multitude of daily tasks that are part of work in the home.

Many practical suggestions and ideas have been brought together in a compact form, organized by subject, so that readers may select topics related to their area of concern. The source for each piece of equipment or device has been indicated for the potential purchaser. This "supermarket" of ideas for persons with disabilities and those who wish to do the job in an easier way should be in every home reference library. These ideas translate to new capabilities for everyone.

Lois O. Schwab, Ed.D.
Professor
Independent Living Rehabilitation Unit
College of Home Economics
University of Nebraska, Lincoln

PREFACE

This book was compiled from a series of articles published by the *Ames Daily Tribune,* Ames, Iowa. The first article appeared in 1973. The focus is on the needs of elderly and handicapped persons who want to remain independent. Daily routines, household chores, and communications are all part of your living pattern.

Most of the items discussed and pictured can be ordered by mail. Others are to show you an easier way to perform a particular task.

The numbers below each article refer to Section 15 at the back of the book listing names and addresses of the sources for these devices. Most of the companies listed publish a catalogue.

Special attention has been given to the needs of the readers. The spiral binding and the large type should make this handbook easy to read and handle.

The Song of the Aged

There's nothing whatever the matter with me
I'm just as healthy as I can be
I have arthritis in both my knees,
And when I talk, I talk with a wheeze.
My pulse is weak and my blood is thin,
But I'm awfully well for the shape I'm in.

I think my liver is out of whack
And a terrible pain is in my back.
My hearing is poor, my sight is dim.
Most everything seems to be out of trim.
But I'm awfully well for the shape I'm in.

I have arch supports for both my feet
Or I wouldn't be able to go out in the street.
Sleeplessness I have night after night
And in the morning I'm just a sight.
My memory is failing, my head's in a spin,
But I'm awfully well for the shape I'm in.

The moral is this as the tale we unfold,
That for you and me who are growing old,
It's better to say "I'm fine" with a grin,
Than to let them know the shape we're in.

—Thanks to Peg Bowman, Ames, Iowa
Author Unknown

Section 1

Cooking and Cleaning

Kitchen Sink Changes

If you are in a wheelchair or have to work sitting down, give some thought to making your kitchen more convenient. When you sit at the sink to work, you need open space below to allow your knees and feet to rest comfortably. Remove the doors from the undersink cabinets to give you this space. Some undersink cabinets have a floor elevated above the kitchen floor. This makes a resting place for your feet and you can get closer to the sink. Wrap the drainpipes with some kind of insulating material to protect your knees from burns.

A shelf directly above the sink can be used to store your most frequently used tools and utensils. Magnetic racks, pegboards, and narrow shelves can be used to store the things you use first at the sink.

Store items at the point of "first use." Plan carefully the storage of all frequently used utensils from paring knives to cooking pans. Planning saves your energy and helps prevent fatigue.

3

Pegboard for Tools

Opening doors, stooping to reach inside, or stretching for items in high cupboards are all problems for those who must work from a wheelchair, walker, or while balancing crutches. Most kitchens have someplace where a pegboard could be installed on a wall. This makes frequently used utensils and tools easily accessible.

The pegboard material and a variety of hooks can be purchased in a lumber yard or hardware store. Efficient use of a pegboard is increased when placed near the kitchen sink because almost all food preparation begins in the sink area where water is available. This saves trips around the kitchen and thus time and energy.

Source: 19, 38

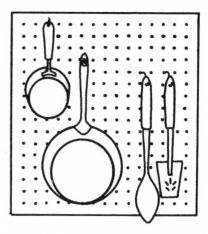

Accessible Corner Cupboards

Do you have a cupboard that goes into an inaccessible corner? Maddening, isn't it? You can make this corner useable with the addition of a simple lazy-Susan shelf.

You can purchase a round lazy-Susan shelf with either one or two shelves at a hardware or variety store. This will fit into a cupboard, refrigerator, cabinet, or on a counter top. It is a great place to store all kinds of small, easily lost items such as spices, food colorings, instant coffee, seasonings, or, in another location, cleansing compounds, window cleaners, and furniture polish.

Make all your cupboards completely useful. Add a turn-around shelf and refrain from griping about those "dead" corners. If you can rotate the items, you can find them and use them. This turns a "nothing" space into a "something" space.

Source: 19, 36

Sink Board

The sink is the center of the work area in the kitchen and the average homemaker spends many hours a week at the sink, preparing vegetables and fruits or washing dishes. Having the bottom of the sink at the most comfortable height for you personally can relieve the strain resulting from using a surface that is too low.

To test your sink for correct working height, sit or stand in front of it with elbows straight but relaxed. In this position, the palms of your hands should rest comfortably on the bottom of the sink. If the sink is too low, you can become overtired.

A simple homemade wooden device can be used to elevate the dishpan or other containers used in the sink. You can decide the most comfortable height for yourself. Two boards a bit shorter than the width of the sink and from six to eight slats are the needed materials. Either nail or screw the slats on the horizontal lifters for an inexpensive back saver.

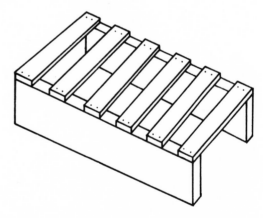

Soap Dispensing Sponge

For those of you who live alone or even for a couple, a few dishes to wash after a meal seem unworthy of a dishpan full of soapsuds. This sponge scrubber does the job with ease.

The hollow handle is filled with liquid detergent. As you hold the dishes under the hot-water tap, the detergent feeds into the sponge, making suds to adequately clean the plates and cups and even pots and pans. If you feel that scalding water is necessary to disinfect the dishes, stack them in the sink drainer and rinse them with water from the teakettle. Allow them to air-dry. It's quicker and more sanitary than using a dish towel.

Source: 14, 36

Small Dish Drainer

For a household of one or two persons, this small dish drainer that fits over just a part of the sink is a space saver and should help make quick work of the daily dish cleanup.

This drainer holds plates, glasses, and silverware and can be placed over the sink so that you need only to rinse the dishes and let them air-dry.

This drainer also doubles as a holder for fruits and vegetables to be rinsed off under the water tap. Use it to place frozen foods to thaw and prevent the drip on the counter top. It takes up a minimum of space under the sink.

Source: 14, 19, 36

Bottle and Jar Openers

Opening jars, bottles, or glass containers can be difficult even for the ablebodied. For those with hand or muscle weakness the task is often impossible.

These two openers are designed to unscrew a lid with a mimimum of effort. One mounts on the wall, the other under a cabinet, so they take up little space and are readily available. Either one is efficient and easily operated, even with one hand.

Source: 11, 14, 16, 20, 24, 29, 37

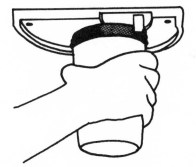

One-handed Juice Opener

Homemakers who are disabled in some way, especially those who have limitation of strength in arms or hands or the use of only one hand, are always looking for an easier way to perform routine kitchen tasks.

To puncture a tall juice can, open a drawer, place the can inside the drawer, and lean on the drawer with your hip to keep the can firm. You can easily use a puncture type opener to make the holes in the can.

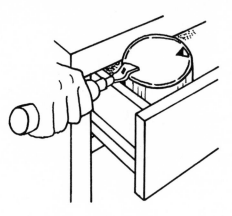

One-handed Can Opener

Most homemakers use many canned foods but may not be able to use a conventional can opener. Dozens of electric can openers are on the market, but shop carefully. Ask yourself and the dealer these questions.

Does the puncturing device operate with a minimum of pressure?

Does the can opener hold the can securely while cutting?

Is the cutting device removable for cleaning? (They say the cutting disc is the dirtiest inch in your kitchen.)

Is there a magnet to hold the lid after removal?

Does the opener leave smooth edges on both the can and lid?

Is it easy to remove the can after it is opened?

Can you operate the appliance with only one hand?

Do the appliance and the cord have the Underwriters Laboratory (UL) seal of approval?

Source: 19, 20

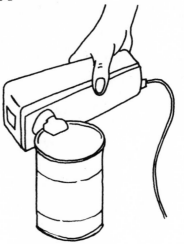

Clip-on Lap Tray

Homemakers who spend most of their time in a wheelchair or need to sit down to do their kitchen work have very special problems that persons not so afflicted fail to understand. Tables or counters are too high, the arms of the chair interfere with the tabletop, and finding a comfortable work area is difficult.

This clip-on lap tray is made of heavy, waterproof, plastic-coated fabric. The tray fits around the waist like an apron, but the plastic waist band requires no fastener or tie and fits any size. The edge is raised 1 1/2 inches to prevent food parings and small articles from rolling to the floor. The plastic is washable and can be kept clean and sanitary for daily use in food preparation.

Source: 39

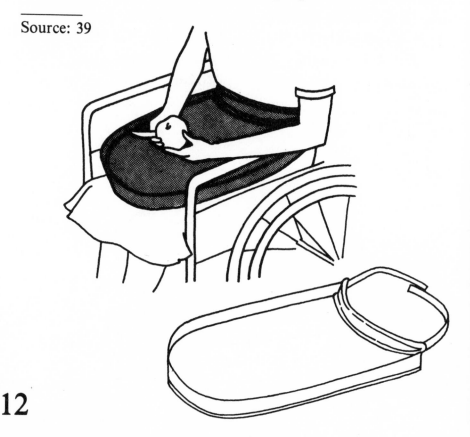

Portable Hand Mixer

A portable hand mixer is a welcome addition to most any kitchen but is especially appreciated by those who have limited strength in their hands and arms. There are many kinds on the market and prices vary from $10 to $30.

Before you buy, check these features. It should be easy to hold, not too heavy, and well balanced when in use. The beater blades should be easy to install and remove for cleaning. Check to be sure the mixer can be operated with only one hand, including the on-off switch and speed control.

The controls should be easy to read and marked in such a way that the numbers do not rub off. The cord may be attached or detachable but should be made of waterproof material.

It is wise to buy a mixer with enough power to perform the jobs you will use it for. One with too small a motor may overheat when beating heavy batters. Check to be sure the appliance has the UL seal.

Source: 19

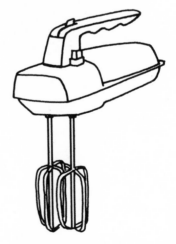

13

Egg Separator

There are many egg separators on the market, all designed to assist the cook with that tricky job of separating the yolk from the white of the egg.

This one is made of glazed earthenware and has a slot in the side. Just crack the egg into the bowl and tilt toward the slot. The white slides out, leaving the yolk intact.

If you should break a yolk and have a speck or two in the white, the eggshell is the best tool for removing the yolk. The affinity is great and the yolk slips right onto the edge of the cracked shell—much easier than onto a spoon or other utensil.

Source: 1, 14, 19, 38

Suction Cups to Steady Bowls

When you are trying to beat eggs, whip cream, mix dough, or stir batter, it is often difficult to keep the mixing bowl steady enough to complete the job. Persons with only one hand or with limited grasp find suction holders a big help.

These are made of soft rubber with 24 tiny suction cups on each side. These suction cups provide a double-acting grip to anchor dishes, glasses, bowls, or containers of food on a lap or bed tray. A mixing bowl is kept from slipping and sliding during food preparation.

Suction cups usually come three to a package and can be purchased in variety stores and some grocery stores. They can also be used as a soap holder in the sink or lavatory, as the water can drain from the soap and keep it dry.

Source: 19, 20, 36

Cutting Board

Peeling a potato or slicing a roast presents an almost impossible task for a person with the use of only one hand. A cutting board such as the one illustrated will be a big help if you have this problem.

Any hardwood board can serve the purpose. Have someone drive two or three rustproof nails through the bottom of the board. These spikes impale the vegetable for peeling or the meat for slicing. You may also want to put suction cups on the bottom to keep it firmly in place during use. One can equip a corner with a slightly elevated edge and the same device serves as a sandwich-making board.

This item can be homemade or it can be ordered by mail.

Source: 16, 20

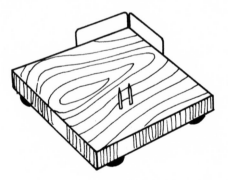

Easy-to-use Vegetable Peeler

Many arthritic patients and others with limited grasp, experience difficulty when peeling vegetables such as potatoes or carrots. The handles of the peelers or knives are too small to hold securely.

This easy-grip peeler solves that problem for you. All the fingers of your hand fit around the handle, and the blade turns a bit to accommodate the angle of the vegetable. One small, sharp blade protrudes above the floating blade to remove potato eyes or bad spots.

Most hardware and variety stores carry this item.

Source: 19, 20, 36

Chopper Bowl

Another help for those with the use of only one hand! This large hardwood bowl with a four-bladed chopper can be used for chopping cabbage, onions, or other vegetables and fruits.

The bowl is 10 1/2 inches in diameter and will not tip even when food is chopped vigorously. The wood is treated with a sealer for stain resistance and long wear.

The blades of the chopper are shaped to fit the bowl for solid contact with the food being processed. This makes a useful addition to any kitchen.

Source: 20

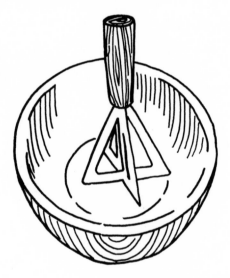

Pizza Cutter

A weakened grasp from an accident or disease can make it very difficult to cut or dice foods. Also, persons with the use of only one hand would find this tool useful in many kitchen related jobs.

It is really a pizza cutter but is adaptable for many other cutting jobs. The blade should be made of good quality stainless steel. As you move the cutter back and forth across the food, the blade rotates and cuts or chops. A larger than normal handle makes this utensil easy for many people to use.

Most hardware and some grocery stores stock this cutter. The cost is modest and should be a welcome addition to many kitchens.

Source: 19, 20

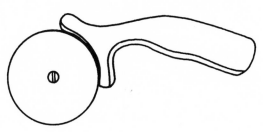

Nonskid Bowl

At last a lightweight, one-handed, nonskid mixing bowl. This permits one-handed stirring. A soft rubber ring is attached to the bottom that prevents skidding and slipping. It is not a vacuum cup. The handle permits easy pouring to transfer the cake batter to the baking pan.

Bowls come in different sizes and are made of colorful plastic, so you can match your kitchen decor. They usually can be found at your local hardware store or gourmet kitchen shop.

Source:19

Mark Range Switches

Most of us lose some visual acuity as we grow older. One kitchen hazard of poor eyesight concerns the switches on either the gas or electric range. Most everyone wants to continue to be independent and perform daily routines. You who are especially concerned about a parent or friend can perform a real service by making the switches more easily read.

Mark the position on the switch for low, medium, and high in large initials with bright colored paint or nail polish. Plastic lettering tape with adhesive backing also works. This method may be used on any surface unit or burner as well as on the oven control. They could be color coded such as red for hot, yellow for medium, and blue or green for low. Be sure to mark the OFF position also.

Those of us who still function at an average level of efficiency must be ever mindful of the problems faced daily by those who suffer "the insults of aging."

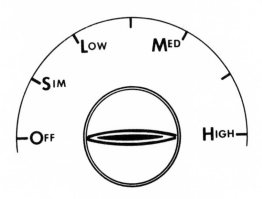

Switch Turner

Arthritic patients encounter many difficulties in routine household tasks because the strength of their hands and arms is often very limited. Finding alternative methods of performing daily jobs is a sharing process between these patients and their families.

Pictured here is one device to assist in turning the switches of a kitchen range. The dowel should be large in diameter to provide an easy grasp. The notch in one end can be made the proper size to fit the switches on your range. This added leverage makes turning on the oven or surface units a much simpler job.

For ranges that have switches on the back panel, a longer dowel with a handle inserted in one end makes reaching and turning switches safer and easier.

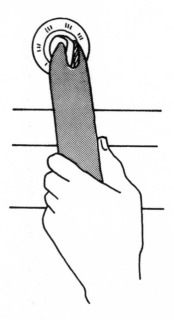

Top-of-range Baker

For you who live alone or cook for two, it seems very wasteful in these days of the energy crunch to heat an entire oven to bake a potato, or an apple, or to heat a few rolls.

This stove-top baker can save energy as it uses only 1/12th the heat of an oven. You can use it on either gas or electric ranges and it does all kinds of small baking jobs.

The cooker is made of chrome-plated steel; it's easy to use and bakes a satisfactory product.

Source: 14, 16, 26

French-fry Basket

For many homemakers, especially those with limited grasp or weak arm muscles, lifting a pan with liquid to or from the range is hazardous.

Place the pan on the range and pour the water into it with a smaller utensil or a cup. When cooking vegetables, spaghetti, macaroni, and other foods that need to be drained, use a French-fry basket.

These wire baskets can be bought in a set with a pan that fits or separately to use in a pan you have. There is usually some device to balance the basket for draining on the edge of the pan. By letting the liquid drain back into the cooking utensil, the homemaker does not have to lift the heavier pan with hot water. Try to do the kitchen tasks easily and safely.

Source: 19, 34

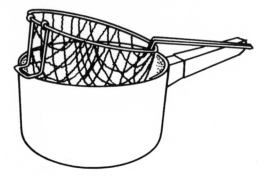

Steady Cooking Utensils

Cooks who have the use of only one hand often find solutions to their problems that are adaptable for use by anyone. A handle holder for a cooking pan can be made quickly from materials that are easy to obtain. This device steadies a hot saucepan on the range while the person preparing the food stirs the contents.

Materials needed are two pieces of 1/2-inch plywood (4 inches by 5 inches and 2 1/2 inches by 5 1/2 inches) and three screw-on suction cups. The boards may be covered with formica or painted but that is not necessary.

The upright piece of wood has a slot cut in it about the size of the usual saucepan handle. Fasten the upright securely to the base, screw on the suction cups, and the job is finished. This keeps the pan from turning as you stir.

Source: 16, 20

Picking Up Pans

Persons with arthritis do not have to be told to save their joints and do housework the easy way. They know how painful it can be when they put too much strain and weight on the sensitive arm and hand joints.

Hospital therapists suggest using two hands to pick up cooking utensils. Use the palms, not the fingers. If you observe the two illustrations, it is obvious that the two-handed method of lifting pots and pans enables a person to use the stronger joint, not the weak and crippled fingers. You will also note the hand is protected by a padded mitt. These are available in department stores for a nominal price.

Double Handle Pots

Those of you who suffer from arthritis know that you are supposed to treat yourself gently and avoid as much strain on your joints and muscles as possible. Therapists caution arthritics about lifting and give suggestions for balancing the load when carrying various items.

This item, a double handle for a cooking pot, enables a person to use both hands to lift a kettle to the range or remove it. By using both hands you can distribute the weight more evenly and it serves as a precaution against accidents.

This handle fits around the pot and screws tightly to form an extra lifter. The source of supply offers directions for making this or you can buy it at a reasonable price.

Source: 23

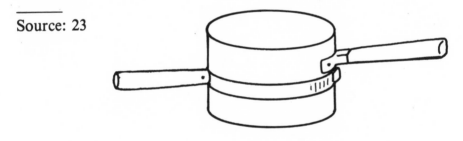

Lifting Techniques

Persons suffering from arthritis learn by experience the right and wrong ways of performing various household tasks. The right way saves energy and is not painful to the affected joints. These sketches illustrate techniques that are taught to arthritic patients.

It is helpful to avoid using fingers to lift plates, trays, or heavy roasting pans. By using padded mitts for protection from heat, you can lift with the palms of the hands and let the stronger wrists and elbows do the work. This method saves the strain on crippled fingers and is more efficient.

Another suggestion is to avoid lifting whenever possible. Slide the pan or dish along the counter top if the design of your kitchen allows this method. Again, use the palms of the hands rather than fingers.

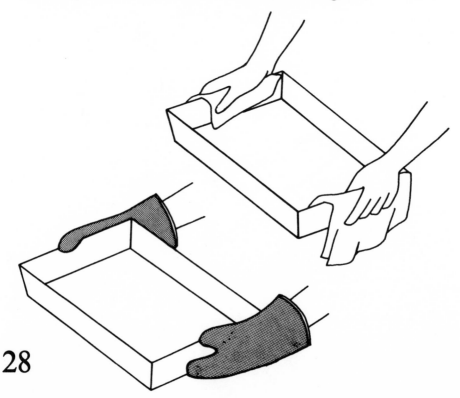

28

Flour Sifters

Many of you who have some limitations on the use of your arms and hands still continue to cook and bake for yourselves or your families. Sifting flour presents different problems to different people, depending on their physical disabilities. If you have the use of only one hand, but it is still strong, the one-handed sifter with a grip handle may work for you.

For some homemakers, the "old-fashioned" sifter with the rotating handle works much easier. It requires little effort to turn the handle and these sifters are usually less expensive than the one-handed, triple-sift variety.

With the use of only one hand and limited grasp, an ordinary sieve can also do the job. This requires only a back and forth motion of the arm to aerate the flour and give an accurate measurement.

Source: 20, 37

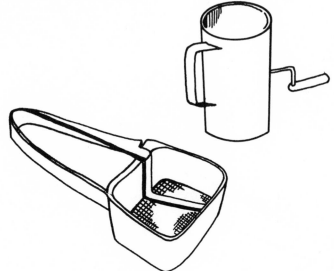

29

One-handed Rolling Pin

Those of you who have the use of only one hand, do not be discouraged. There is a rolling pin that will enable you to roll pizza, bread, cookies, or piecrust. It's design is similar to that of a paint roller, except the roller part is wooden. You can use it for any kind of rolling process as you create your kitchen delicacies.

Inexpensive, versatile, and efficient, this tool can be a real boon to a cook who has lost the use of a hand or the strength of one arm. It may be just what you need to regain your efficiency on the breadboard.

Source: 19, 20

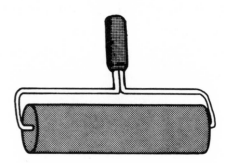

One-handed Cookie Dropper

When you make cookies for your family or grand-children, it is often difficult and messy to spoon the cookie batter onto the baking sheet. This ejector spoon is great.

Scoop the batter on the spoon, push the lever on the handle, and the dough is placed exactly where you want it.

This tool works for batter, jam, honey, jelly, peanut butter, shortening, and other foods. It is made of stainless steel and can be washed in the dishwasher. It eliminates gooey fingers, saves utensils, and can be used with only one hand.

Source: 14

Flip-open Spatula

The usual spatula is often too small or narrow to do the big jobs at the kitchen range. This automatic flip-open spatula spreads to 9 inches wide. You place the folded-up spatula under a cake, fish, pancakes, or omelet and then flick the lever. With the spatula's wide spread, you can lift large and sometimes awkward objects from the pan or skillet.

This useful utensil is made of stainless steel, so it cleans easily and gives long service.

Source: 13, 38

Giant Fork Lifters

Is it hard for you to lift a heavy piece of meat or a roast? Sometimes, especially when the meat is very hot, it is difficult to lift the meat onto a platter or serving dish.

This pair of giant forks makes a problem job into an easy task. Made of heavy-duty steel with solid wooden handles, the forks measure 12 inches. The tines are broad enough to allow meat juices to drop back into the cooking pan. Thongs tied through the handles let you hang the forks, saving drawer space.

Source: 14, 34, 38

Beverage Container
for Refrigerator

When most of us are thirsty, we go to the sink, turn on the tap, and get a glass of water. However, there are those who have trouble reaching the faucet, turning it on, or even holding a glass.

This container for the refrigerator can eliminate this problem and lets you have cold water, juice, or milk handy all the time. It measures 5 1/2 inches by 13 inches by 4 inches and is made of sturdy unbreakable plastic. Fit it on any shelf in your refrigerator and you eliminate grasping, lifting, and pouring.

Source: 11, 26

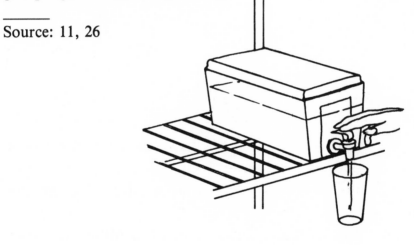

Milk Carton Opener

Are you ever frustrated trying to open one of the waxed milk cartons? A great deal of pressure is required.

This three-pronged tool is designed especially to pry open the milk carton. The handle is extra large for easier grasp. Just fit it into the side of the carton marked "open here" and a simple prying movement quickly breaks the seal.

Of course this would work on cream or half-and-half cartons also.

Source: 23

Milk Carton Holder

Arthritics and others who have a very limited grasp find lifting a milk carton, either quart or half-gallon, very difficult. The person's hand is often not strong enough to actually secure a good grip on the container. When milk is spilled, it seems to cover a very large area of the kitchen or dining room floor.

A special holder is available for various sizes of square cartons. It actually makes an easy-pour pitcher out of the milk carton. Made of tough plastic, it is almost unbreakable, and can be boiled or washed in the dishwasher.

They are often available in hardware and variety stores but can be ordered by mail.

Source: 14, 36

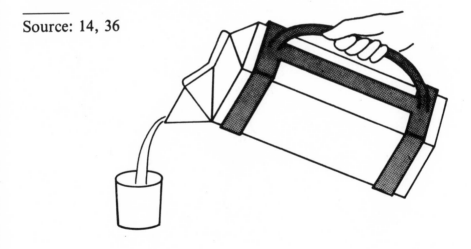

Crutch Patient's Apron

People who use crutches to assist in walking have great difficulty carrying anything, because hands are required to manipulate the crutches. This apron can serve as a carryall for homemakers who continue to do their own housework.

The apron is made of a combination of terry cloth for absorption of liquids, plastic for protection inside the pockets, and attractive corded fabric for the pocket exterior. The apron fastens with a gripper-type fabric fastener to avoid the task of tying.

You can carry the dust cloth, window cleaner, furniture polish, and other cleaning equipment. Save one pocket to pick up misplaced items around your home.

Source: 39

Long-handled Tub Scrubber

Cleaning the bathtub or under a counter or table are difficult tasks to perform when you lose mobility. Persons who have difficulty bending or stooping also find these chores burdensome—to say the least.

A long-handled no-bend sponge is the answer. There are many types on the market and the cost varies. Some have wooden handles, others are lightweight metal, and the sponge is firmly attached for long wear. If the handle is too small, you can build it up with sponge rubber or foam taped in place with water-resistant tape.

Source: 14, 16, 17, 19, 20, 23, 26

Long-handled Duster

To dust or not to dust can be a difficult question. To help you with this chore, buy a long-handled duster. You can dust both high and low places with one of these tools, even from a sitting position.

Some dusters are made of natural wool fibers; others are made of sponge or have fabric covers that are removable for washing. You can reach high places such as windows, doors, or lamps, as well as baseboards or shelves. Some are slim enough to go behind radiators or furniture. A little commercial spray to attract the dust is helpful.

Source: 11, 13, 26, 37, 38

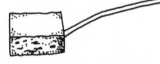

Cobweb Catcher

Cobwebs become a real nuisance certain times of the year, especially in corners near the ceiling. This inexpensive gadget can be attached to your kitchen broom, allowing you to reach the highest or lowest parts of your house to wipe away the webs.

The cover is fluffy orlon acrylic. It gathers and holds dust and lint as well as cobwebs. It won't scratch or smudge the walls, either.

This washable cover fastens with a drawstring over any standard broom.

Source: 14

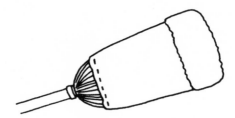

Helps for Hand Laundry

For people who have a limited grasp because of an accident or arthritis, doing hand laundry such as lingerie can be nearly impossible.

To wash clothing by hand, such as lingerie or fine garments, make suds in a bucket, put in the clothing, and agitate it with a small rubber plunger. You can buy one with a short handle. Use the same method for rinsing in clear water.

Try looping the garment around the kitchen faucet and twist a bit to remove some of the excess water. Or roll it in a terry cloth towel to remove even more moisture. This method saves the strain on sore or crippled hands.

Source: 19

Duster-sweeper Broom

Here is a solution to the problem of dusting base-boards or the floors around the edge of rugs. This duster broom acts as both a dust mop and broom. Electrostatic action picks up every speck of dust and dirt.

The head is washable and may be used either dry or damp. The angled head lets you get under furniture and into corners. The handle makes it possible to dust low or high places without stooping or stretching.

Source: 16

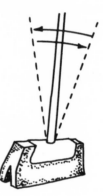

Small Sweeper for Small Jobs

Cleaning tasks never end, or so it seems. Sometimes it is not convenient to get out the vacuum to sweep up a few crumbs. This new little carpet sweeper is perfect for all kinds of small jobs around the home, boat, camper, or car.

It sweeps up sand, dust, ashes, and crumbs from any carpeted, upholstered, or cloth surface. This sweeper is handy to use. Because of its size, 3 inches by 5 inches, you can use it in tight corners, such as on stairways or behind the toilet in the bathroom. You can even crumb the tablecloth. The brushes are made of natural bristles, which are more efficient than synthetic types.

Source: 19, 27, 38

Nonstooping Foot Mop

How do you wipe up spills on the floor when you cannot stoop or bend over? A "foot mop" is a great idea. This mop provides a no-bend way to wipe up kitchen and bathroom spills. It can also be used to dust floors when sprayed with a commercial product made especially to attract dust particles.

The mop is made of absorbent terry cloth and is about 11 inches in diameter with a slip pocket for your foot. Leave it on the floor or in the corner for the next accident. This item is machine washable and requires no special care other than laundering.

Source: 16

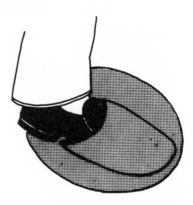

Ironing Made Easier

We all know that the new fabrics have almost eliminated ironing of household linens, men's shirts, ladies' dresses, and even handkerchiefs. However, some of you still have pressing or ironing jobs that need to be done. We don't just get rid of older things, and some new fabrics need a touch-up occasionally.

If you have arthritis or some other physical problem, the weight of a heavy iron is too taxing on the arms and hands. There is at least one iron made that is so light and easy to use that almost anyone with reduced physical strength can manage it. The iron is convertible from dry to steam with the addition of a small plastic bulb that holds ordinary tap water. This iron is listed as a travel iron, but I use it for all kinds of home pressing and ironing jobs.

Source: 19, 26

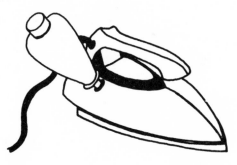

Steam-iron Cover

We all have to do some pressing at times. If you have hand problems, arranging a pressing cloth, spraying it with water, and then ironing the garment becomes a tedious task.

A cover that fits over your steam iron and allows the iron to glide easily over the fabric, dress, trousers, or skirt eliminates much of the fuss and bother. This cover reduces the possible shine on the surface of the garment and prevents the heavier portions such as seams and pockets from showing after pressing.

Source: 14

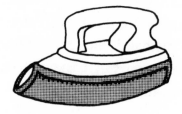

Short-bladed Knife

Opening packages in this modern day where everything comes in boxes, cardboard, or plastic wrap can be a critical problem for any consumer, even those without a physical handicap. Soap boxes are one example, as are some kinds of cake mixes, cereals, and household cleaners. Many of us have trouble getting them open.

You can buy a short-bladed utility knife, the kind used by stock boys in grocery stores. The handle is large enough for a person with limited grasp to hold safely. The blade is sharp and easy to use. Keep one handy in your kitchen and one in your laundry room. Some have retractable blades and I would recommend this type for safety's sake. This tool is much safer than using a paring knife or other tool because the angle of the blade makes it more versatile.

Source: 19

Storage Cart on Wheels

This storage cart on wheels with three baskets and a shelf is a great idea to serve as extra storage, or to roll around with you as you do your cooking or other housework. It fits in a narrow space (10 inches) for extra roll-out storage, and rolls to the table or even outdoors with all you need to set the table or serve a meal. The tray on top lifts off and serves as a storage area as you clear the table.

Use this roll cart to hold all your cleaning cloths, sponges, cleanser, window cleaner, and furniture polish while you clean your house. We all try to save energy and time, and this cart will help.

Source: 11, 13, 38

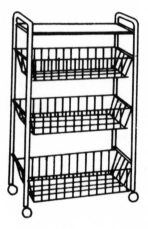

Wringing a Cloth

For those of you who have arthritis that especially affects your hands, the frequent daily chore of wringing a cloth is painful or perhaps impossible.

A hospital therapist offers this solution. For a starting position (Figure 1), hold the cloth parallel to knuckles as shown, with your elbows bent. Then (Figure 2) straighten your arms forward. DO NOT move hand or wrist—the cloth, not the hand, will twist. Clever, isn't it?

Another solution is to twist a cloth around a faucet or water tap to wring it out. All of us who keep house need to use damp cloths frequently and people with arthritis need to know how to protect their hands.

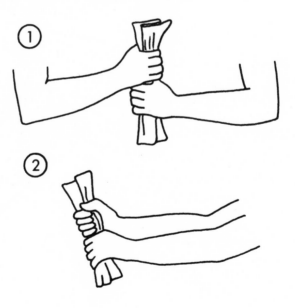

Rolling Saucer

For those of you who have trouble lifting a scrub bucket as you move around the kitchen to clean the floor, this saucer on rollers could be a big help. It is 2 inches deep to catch and hold any spills and is made of heavy plastic sturdy enough to hold a bucket with water in it.

There are other types of rolling stands on the market, but this is more practical than some because of the rim. This same saucer can be used to move large house plants to different locations in your home.

The inside diameter of the saucer is 11 1/2 inches and should accommodate most pots or buckets. The casters are freewheeling to allow a person without much strength to move it along a smooth floor.

Source: 11, 14, 26, 35

Long-handled Tongs

Retrieving articles from the floor or a high shelf concerns many persons who for some reason have limited reach.

On the market are many kinds of long-handled tongs that extend the reach. You can pick up a dropped handkerchief or sock and also reach a cereal box from a high shelf. Some are designed to use with a two-handed grasp; others have a pistol grip for one-handed operation. Others have magnetic tips so you can pick up metal objects.

A handyman in the house can create tongs made of wood. Felt glued to the gripper part ensures a sure grasp of the misplaced item. Try them out before you buy to make sure the design fits your needs.

Source: 16, 20, 26

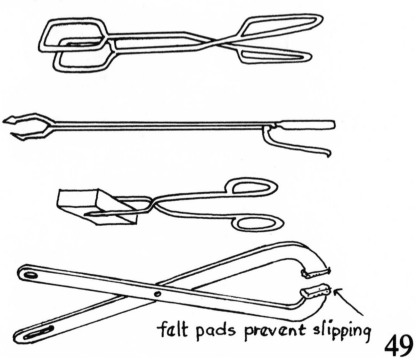

felt pads prevent slipping

Folding Stool

You know that it is dangerous to climb on a chair to reach a high cupboard, yet many people do just that and have serious accidents resulting from this careless practice.

A small folding step stool that can be tucked away behind a door or between appliances is much safer. The stool has two wide, skid-resistant steps and locks firmly in place when opened. The steel frame gives stability. The folded width is only 1 1/2 inches.

Think about your own safety and don't take a chance on a makeshift step stool.

Source: 13, 14, 16, 26

Section 2

The Bathroom

Bathtub Grab Bars

A large variety of safety grab bars can be purchased to install in any bathroom. Older persons and those with limited mobility feel insecure in the tub or shower. You can add one of these bars to compensate for any deteriorating physical or mental abilities.

The bathroom is a particularly vulnerable place for slips and falls. Install one or more bars beside the tub. There are many sizes and shapes and you can find one to fit your situation. Check with a plumbing shop or a hospital supply store. Be sure that they are installed properly, for a loose grab bar is worse than none at all. Be safe.

Source: 16, 20, 29, 30, 40

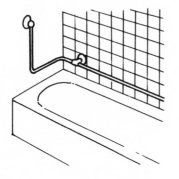 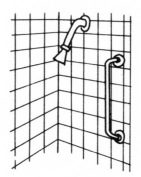

Bathtub Grip Bar

Bathing may well be the most hazardous activity that a handicapped or elderly person tries to do. Getting in or out of the tub is often impossible and can be dangerous if one's footing is insecure.

There are many kinds of security grip bars that can be installed on the bathtub. This device gives persons who are unsteady on their feet a firm place to grasp and the necessary leverage to lift themselves out of the tub. This bar does not take up too much room, is easy to install, and may be purchased from your local pharmacy, hospital supply firm, or plumbing shop.

These bars are made from high-strength anodized aluminum and come with fasteners for proper installation. Most have rubber or plastic padding to prevent scarring of the tub surface.

Source: 1, 11, 14, 30, 33, 34, 35, 37

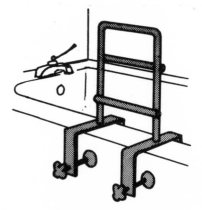

Hand-held Shower Head

Most older homes do not have built-in showers but a personal shower is available that can help solve this problem. These devices are often called "telephone" showers because the head resembles a hand telephone.

The faucet usually has to be changed to install a personal shower. The flexible hose fits on the new faucet. You can direct soothing hot water to any part of the body. For conventional showering, the hand shower may be placed on its adjustable wall bracket at any height you prefer.

The hoses are either flexible chrome-plated brass or reinforced vinyl and are long lasting. The length varies from 40 inches to 70 inches. Some shower heads are designed with push-button volume control for hand-held use.

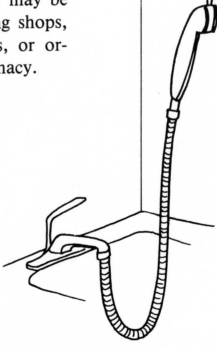

This type of shower may be purchased from plumbing shops, sick-room supply houses, or ordered through your pharmacy.

Source: 30, 36

Bathtub Seat

Bathtub seats can be a help for many people who experience difficulty in getting into or out of a tub. They come in a variety of styles.

One is called a transfer seat and this allows a person to enter a tub by sitting down and lifting the legs over one at a time. One may then either bathe or shower. Other models fit inside a tub and come in heights from 9 inches to 17 inches from tub to seat. Some models are adjustable. One model fits into the tub and is supported wedgelike by the inside of the slanting tub itself.

Depending on your disability, at least one of these models should serve your needs and make it possible for you to bathe safely and more easily.

Source: 13, 14, 16, 29, 30, 33, 35, 37

Shower Seat

The problems of bathing when one is unable to get into a bathtub or stand in a shower plagues many elderly and disabled people. Consider buying a shower seat. This makes it possible for the patient to sit securely in a shower stall and to bathe with minimal effort.

The portable model has 3-inch rubber suction cups that grip the floor and can be placed at any convenient spot in the shower.

A folding unit attaches to the wall and can be lifted out of the way when other persons use the shower. These stools are made of anodized aluminum with a plastic seat, and they do not rust or corrode.

Shower seats can be purchased from plumbing shops and some mail-order catalogues.

Source: 30, 40

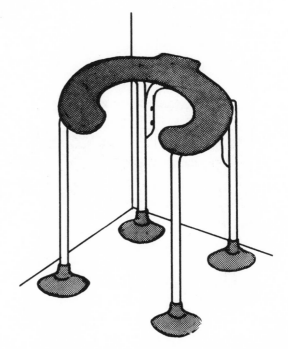

Shower Nonslip Carpet

The cushioned polyurethane foam pad can serve as a carpet for your shower stall. This may help to prevent accidents. It is 24 inches square and has a hole to fit over the drain.

The pad is nonskid and machine washable and dryable. This will help to eliminate any mildew problem that might occur. Between uses the pad can be rolled and placed in a corner of the shower to drain and drip dry.

Source: 13, 26, 34

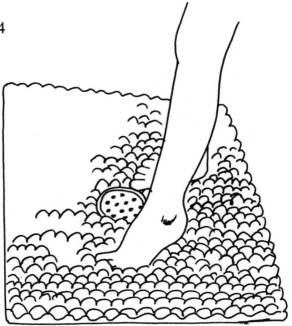

Bath Mattress

People who enjoy a long soaking bath but find the hard porcelain surface of the tub uncomfortable might find this idea a great help.

It is a soft polyethylene foam pad to help make the tub more comfortable. The surface is nonskid, which adds protection for those who may be a bit shaky or unsteady on their feet.

The size is adequate for most bathtubs, 36 inches by 20 inches. The material does not mildew or retain odors; best of all, it is machine washable. Enjoy!

Source: 11, 13, 14, 26, 34

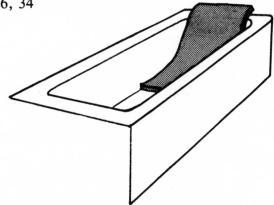

Back Scrubber

Bathing difficulties plague many of our elderly citizens. Getting your back scrubbed is a rather common problem and this solution should help many of you.

The soap fits into a natural rubber sponge and gives abundant suds. The 17-inch handle allows you to reach your back and feet, whether in a shower or tub. The soap is placed in a pocket in the sponge, and you may use small scraps of soap that are usually thrown away. You save soap and keep clean.

Source: 14, 16

Shower Caddy

An addition to the bathrooms of disabled people that will assist them in independent living is a shower caddy. This device hooks onto the shower head and has compartments or shelves to hold soap, shampoo, hand brush, and a washcloth. All the necessities for a shower are within easy reach without stooping or bending.

The cost is minimal. Some are made of aluminum, others of plastic-coated wire or molded plastic. Whatever you buy, it should not rust or corrode. Most hardware and variety stores carry this caddy.

Source: 14, 19, 26, 36, 37, 38

Foot Washer

Washing your legs and feet is most difficult when your reach is restricted or legs are stiff and sore. You can make or buy a gadget for this purpose. The toe washer consists of a long-handled device covered with a terry cloth bag, made like a slip cover. After washing, you can slip a dry terry cloth bag over the end to dry your toes.

To create your own, buy a long-handled rubber or plastic bowl scraper and attach an extra handle of wood or aluminum to make it long enough to reach your feet. Make the terry cloth bags from toweling 5 inches by 5 inches. A heading of elastic or a drawstring holds this in place for washing or drying.

Source: 23

Sling Towel

A sling towel may be easily created by anyone who can sew. This towel enables you to dry your back and other parts of the body when limited reach or strength prohibits the use of a regular towel.

Use terry toweling 36 inches by 18 inches and two pieces of nylon tape measuring 22 inches by 1/2 inch.

To make this towel, fold the terry cloth lengthwise. Stitch around three edges; turn inside out and stitch the remaining end with the edges turned under. Attach the tapes securely to the ends as shown.

This suggestion was offered by the Canadian Arthritis Society.

Safety Bath Strips

What nicer thing can you do for your parents or relatives than to help make their home safer? So many accidents happen in the home and many of them are avoidable with proper equipment or precaution.

You can buy bathtub or shower strips to place in the tub or shower. The rough surface helps to prevent the "slippies" while bathing. An adhesive backing provides easy installation.

Some are strips, others are flowers or figures. They all serve the same purpose and they do help.

Source: 19, 20, 36

Safety Slippers

For those of you who may feel insecure in the shower, these safety slippers should offer you confidence. They are made of nylon net with a special nonskid sole.

The source listed gives sizes only for women, up to 9 1/2. The cost is reasonable, and they are comfortable. I suppose they could double as a bedroom slipper, but they are primarily for use in showers, swimming pools, or locker rooms. Do all you can to make bathing a safe activity.

Source: 14, 26, 37, 38

Elevated Toilet Seat

The daily toilet routine is probably one of the most difficult for a person suffering from acute arthritis or general muscle weakness due to aging. Many persons who presently require assistance in the bathroom could be independent if an elevated toilet seat were added.

You can purchase a seat that fits over the regular toilet seat. Some styles are adjustable; they vary the height depending on the patient's need. Most are equipped with a riser for the back of the seat as well as a stainless steel shield from the seat to the toilet bowl. Wheelchair patients find the height approximately that of the wheelchair seat, which facilitates transfer.

One model is made of firm plastic and molded to fit the body contours. Hospital supply firms, many pharmacies, and some plumbing shops carry elevated toilet seats.

Source: 16, 20, 29, 30, 33

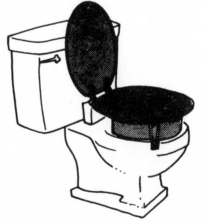

Toilet-safety Rail

Another device providing safety and independence in bathroom routines for the invalid or elderly is the toilet-safety rail.

These devices are made of either chrome-plated steel or aluminum tubing and most have plastic arm rests to provide a firm, sure hold. Some can be installed with no special equipment in minutes. A stainless steel clamp is bolted on with the toilet seat and holds the tube firmly.

The front legs rest on rubber or plastic tips and can be tilted to wash the floor and clean around the bowl. There are many models to choose from. Hospital supply firms, plumbing shops, and some pharmacies stock this item.

Source: 16, 20, 29, 30, 33

Portable Toilet for the Disabled

The use of the bathroom presents some of the most critical problems for persons with a physical handicap or for those in wheelchairs. If a home-bound patient cannot get to the bathroom, you can either purchase or rent a portable commode from a hospital supply house or local pharmacy.

Many styles of commodes ensure that at least one model will fill the needs of the patient about whom you are concerned. Most are light in weight and are usually on rollers for movability. The frame is made of rust-proof metal for long use and durability.

Some are designed to look like regular chairs, others are designed to look like toilets. The plastic pail is easily emptied and cleaned. For a prolonged illness, purchase is recommended, but rentals are available for a short-term confinement.

Source: 29, 33, 40

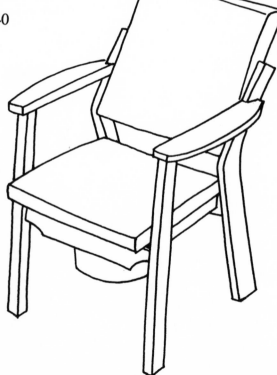

66

Tap Turner

Persons with limited strength have difficulty manipulating water faucets of the four-pronged type. This tool can be a big help. It lessens the strain on fingers and wrist and gives leverage so that a weakened hand can turn the tap on and off.

This device is made of aluminum with wooden handles. The pegs to loosen the faucet are carriage bolts fastened to the aluminum. You can create your own, if you have the aptitude, or they may be ordered ready-made.

This suggestion came from the Canadian Arthritis Society.

Source: 23

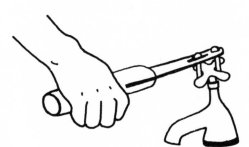

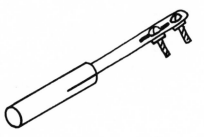

Hand Brushes

Persons with only one hand or limited grasp do experience problems with washing themselves, their dentures, dishes, or vegetables.

Two brushes that may help solve such problems are pictured here. One is fastened to the sink with suction cups and can be used in either the kitchen or bathroom. It can be used for scrubbing knuckles, vegetables, or even some dishes. I would recommend having one each for the kitchen and bathroom.

The other brush fits over the fingers and is useful for those who have little or no finger function. It may also be used in either the bathroom or kitchen. Their cost is low so buy several.

Source: 16, 20, 36

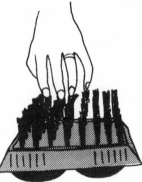

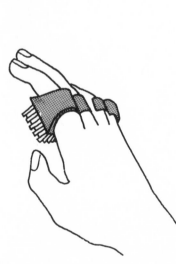

Tube Squeezers

Do you find it difficult to squeeze a tube of toothpaste, shampoo, glue, or makeup? Failing to squeeze the tube in the right place can lead to family arguments.

There are some little devices that can end all that hassle. Either metal or plastic, the slotted roller can be used on any kind of tube.

Just slip the tube into the slit, turn the oversized handle, and the tube decreases in size gradually and neatly. You can use every bit of the contents of the tube. When the tube is finished, unwind and use the roller again. This practice keeps other family members from making snide remarks about your neatness. It is a real boon for crippled hands.

Source: 16, 36, 38

69

Toothbrushes of All Kinds

Personal hygiene is difficult for those who have aches and pains and limited reach. Many specially adapted toothbrushes are available for most any need. Some come with long handles, others with large, easy-grip handles, and one with double brushes to clean both sides of the mouth at once.

Special brushes for dentures are designed for persons with the use of only one hand. They are attached to the lavatory with suction cups.

A catalogue from the resource list offers many solutions to this necessary daily routine.

Source: 20, 23, 29

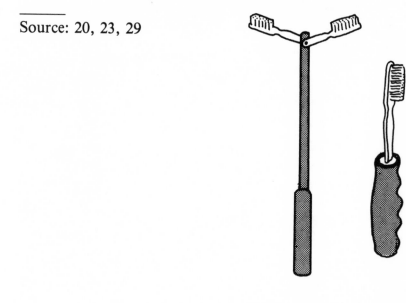

Nonspill Spoons

Taking liquid medicine is never very easy, but for children and some elderly persons it is almost impossible. Holding the spoon, pouring the liquid, and getting the dose into the mouth can be a messy, shaky business.

Available now is a new type of plastic spoon with a hollow vial as a part of the spoon. The vial is marked with measures from 1/4 teaspoon to 2 teaspoons to ensure accurate measurement. By pouring the cough syrup or whatever else you may need to administer into the spoon, you can clearly see the amount. Tip the spoon into the mouth and presto—no spills. This sometimes unpleasant job is accomplished in record time.

The price is modest, so you may afford to buy more than one. A quick rinse under the tap makes it ready for the next time.

Source: 29

Pill-reminder Box

Do you ever forget to take the prescribed medicine or sometimes worse, take it oftener than prescribed?

An inexpensive addition to your medicine cabinet is a pill-reminder box. There are seven compartments, one for each day, with letters on top of the hinged lids to indicate days of the week. You can also purchase this box with Braille markings on the lids for a blind patient.

It is made of unbreakable plastic and is small enough to fit into a purse or pocket. Several colors are available, and if you have many medications, you may want more than one.

Source: 2, 13, 26, 29

Pill-taking Glass

For those of you who have trouble swallowing a pill, this special glass can help solve the problem. It is made of plastic and has a small shelf on which you place the pill or capsule. Small slits guide the water to the pill and your mouth. The whole thing washes down with no choking.

This inexpensive item is recommended for children and adults who experience difficulty in swallowing non-liquid medicine. It works!

Source: 29

Eyedrops

Persons who have to use eyedrops daily or frequently often have visual problems. Trying to see without glasses creates a hazard for those who need eye medicine.

To solve the problem, measure the dosage of eyedrops first (with your glasses on). Lie down or lean back, close your eyes, and release the dropper into the corner of your eye. When you open the eyelid, the drops flow onto the surface of the eye. This method keeps you from flinching and the medicine is directed to the right place. It can be used for children who need eye medications as well as for the mature patient.

Dressing and Grooming

Dowel Pin Aid

For you who suffer from arthritis or a similar ailment, dressing yourself each day is a battle. If you search patiently, you can find clothing designed for persons with physical disabilities.

This idea is applicable for both women and men. Sew loops of cotton tape to the sides of the underwear. Two dowel sticks, with cup hooks in one end, serve as an arm extension to reach the underpants and pull them up over the body. The dowels should be about 2 feet long and the hooks double as hangers to keep them handy.

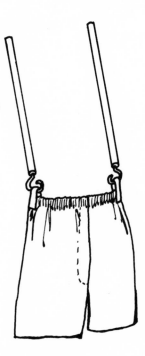

Buttoning Devices

Many arthritis sufferers have particular difficulty in trying to fasten buttons on shirts, or blouses, or dresses, or even coats. The fingers become stiff, swollen or gnarled, and just don't work right.

If you are old enough to remember when we wore high-buttoned shoes, you remember the button hook. The many buttoners on the market work on a similar principle. Slip the wire loop through the buttonhole, hook onto the button, and pull it back through the slit.

This device comes in many styles—long handled, fat handled, or one that fits on the wrist. There is variety enough to solve any need.

Source: 16, 20, 23

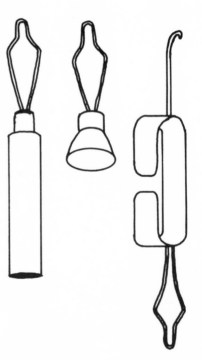

Easy Fasteners

There are many kinds of closures on the market for dresses, shirts, and blouses but persons with limited hand function find buttons, snaps, and hooks and eyes hard to manipulate. You can buy round fasteners of VELCRO® which take the place of other fasteners. A self-sticking surface on this fastener allows the seamstress to sew without basting.

Anyone with limited dexterity will find these round fasteners grip tightly to hold the garment closed but peel apart easily to unfasten the placket.

Source: 15

Clip-on Tie

Even though our dress is more casual than ever before, I am sure that some of you men readers have occasion to dress up with a necktie. With hand or arm limitations, it may be next to impossible to tie a necktie and make the knot look neat. You can buy clip-on ties in adult styles that can be put on with no reaching or tying.

Assuming you can button your shirt, you can put this tie over the collar button and the tabs under the collar—a quick and handsome way to dress up. Ties of this kind are available in men's stores or in the men's departments of other outlets.

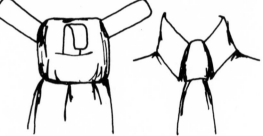

Elastic Thread for Buttons

For arthritics and others with limited finger function, fastening buttons is an arduous task. There are many solutions, but a very easy one is to use elastic thread.

You can buy it in packages or spools and use the thread to attach the button to the blouse or shirt cuff. Keep the cuff buttoned at all times and push your hand through the cuff. The elastic stretches enough to permit this expansion and no one is the wiser.

Poncho-blanket or Cape

The colorful poncho-blanket makes a comfortable wrap to be used by a wheelchair patient or a person with limited arm functon. It also serves indoors as a lap robe or blanket.

The fiber is 100 percent acrylic, machine washable, and shrink resistant. Opening the zipper changes the lap robe into a shoulder wrap. A zippered case is included to carry this multipurpose garment.

The cape is cut below the waist in back to eliminate the bulk of ordinary outer garments. It is made of water-repellent poplin that resists wind and rain and is suitable for either men or women. The front covers the knees and legs,and the hood gives extra protection. You can buy this either lined or unlined and it can be ordered with either an even or uneven hemline.

Source: 16

Custom-designed Clothing

Many of you who suffer from crippling arthritis find it difficult to dress yourself in conventional blouses, dresses, or trousers.

An organization in Cleveland, Ohio, specializes in creating all kinds of clothing for the disabled. You can buy blouses, dresses, slips, robes, trousers (for men or women), aprons, and other items of clothing—all with YOU in mind. If you have special needs, describe the problem and their designers will figure out a solution.

This organization is a member of the Cleveland United Way. Their dedicated personnel go out of their way to assist their many clients.

Garments may be fitted with nylon gripper tape, snaps, zippers, buttons or other fasteners—whatever is easy for you. The choice of material and style allows you to have personalized clothing that specifically fits your needs.

Source: 39

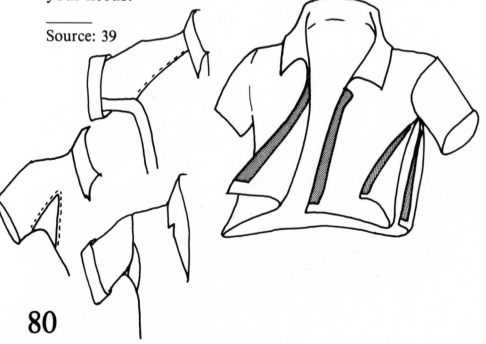

80

Quick-change Dress

The quick-change dress is a creative idea developed at a rehabilitation workshop. It stays neat. Two designs are available, one with a quick-change front panel and one with a quick-change bib. You can choose solid colors or prints, darks or pastels, gingham checks or plaids.

The panels are fastened to the dress with nylon gripper tape, with buttons, or with metal snaps. This garment comes in both children's and adult sizes. It would be most useful for a person who is unsure with eating tools and appropriate, too, for any busy, curious little girl. This dress certainly could save on laundry and help wearers to keep a fresh appearance.

Source: 39

Elastic-top Trousers

Pulling trousers on and off or fastening zippers and belts can be an impossible task for a person with limited grasp and dexterity of the arms and hands. Stroke patients, arthritics, and some with Parkinson's disease share this difficulty.

A proved solution is to alter the trousers with the addition of elastic. Buy the trousers one size larger than is actually needed and place wide (1/2-inch to 3/4-inch elastic around the waistband. Measure the waist and subtract 1 or 2 inches so that when they are sewed, the pants will be taut enough to stay in place at the waist.

Start on the inside of the front placket, pin the elastic even with the top of the pants at both side seams, center back, and on the other side of the front placket, dividing the elastic into approximately fourths to make the gathers evenly divided. Use a zig-zag or stretch stitch on the machine and attach the elastic both top and bottom on the inside of the waistband. As you sew, stretch to fit the space. This does make the waist slightly gathered but also provides a functional answer to a problem shared by many. Leave the button or hook at the top fastened. The trousers can be easily removed and this adjustment solves a personal need for the afflicted. Commercial pants are available.

Source (for ready-made): 16

Easy-dress Slacks

These slacks are available for both women and men. The fabric and color choices are many. Especially for those of you who have trouble with zippers or buttons, the nylon gripper-tape fastener permits easy dressing.

The trousers come in regular sizes, but the organization will make them to fit a person who has unusual measurements. For a person wearing a brace or cast, the slacks can be made with a leg opening for ease in dressing.

Source: 39

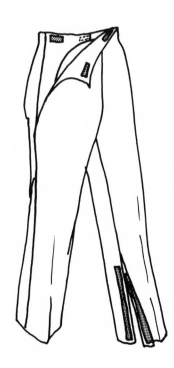

Homemade Tool

Arthritics, wheelchair patients, and others who have limited reach or severe loss of movement will find this simple, homemade device helpful in many ways. Therapy departments of hospitals recommend this tool for many kinds of ailments.

Take a dowel pin about 18 inches long and screw an old-fashioned coat hanger in the end of the dowel. In the other end install a cup hook. This gadget can be used to remove clothes from hooks or hangers in a closet, to take off your socks when you can't reach them, or to pick up objects from the floor.

This tool can help with dozens of daily tasks—turning faucets off or on, pulling up a zipper, or removing a shirt or sweater from your shoulders. The cup hook serves as a hanger.

Source: 16, 20, 23

Long Shoehorn

No matter what kind of shoes you wear, slip-ons or ties, if you can't bend over to use a shoehorn, you may require help in dressing. Persons in wheelchairs, on crutches, in casts, or with bad backs or other disabilities often find this final act of dressing to be a snarl.

Use a long-handled shoehorn. You can put on your shoes from a standing position or when seated. They may be purchased in shoe stores or department stores. Styles vary from plain to fancy and the cost varies accordingly. It is a good idea to get one that will hang on a closet hook so it is handy when you need it.

Source: 16, 20

Shoelaces

When you can't bend over because you are a bit round in the tummy or have the use of only one hand, you simply can't tie your own shoes. There are many aids available for this dressing problem.

Elastic shoelaces are one answer. They can be laced and tied and kept tied. They stretch enough to allow you to put on your own shoes with a minimum of effort and without disturbing the bow.

Others have a plastic slip knot. A fastener of nylon grabtape can be added to some shoe styles. One-handed varieties can be ordered through hospital supply firms.

Source: 16, 20, 29

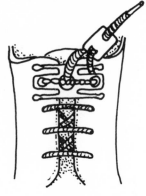 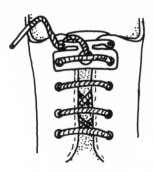

Bootjack

Do you have trouble removing your shoes? A boot-jack can solve this difficulty for a person who cannot bend over or has limited strength. In earlier years military men usually used a gadget like this to remove the high boots they wore with their uniforms. I can see it being used by those of you who wear boots or have a physical problem and can't bend over or stoop.

This jack can be constructed of two pieces of wood. The top piece should be about 13 inches long by 5 inches wide. Nail or screw it to another piece of wood about 1 to 2 inches high. Use one foot to hold it firmly while removing the other shoe.

Source: 20, 23

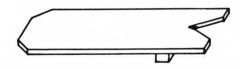

Special Combs

Can you comb your own hair? Personal grooming is a real problem for many who are handicapped. Some need a long-handled comb, others an angled comb, and still others have a grasp problem and need a built-up handle.

You can make your own large-handled comb by gluing a rat-tail comb into a file handle, which can be purchased at your local hardware store. The long-handled or angled combs probably have to be ordered from your local hospital supply house or pharmacy. These self-help devices are especially useful for persons with arthritis or limited use of the hands and arms.

Source: 20, 23, 29

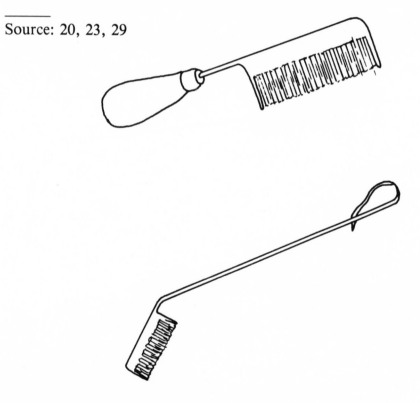

Neck Mirror

Combing your own hair, putting on makeup, and performing other personal grooming tasks that require a mirror can be extremely difficult for a person in a wheelchair or with limited hand dexterity. A neck mirror can help solve the problem.

Using this around-the-neck mirror, you free both hands to perform the necessary chores. You can use this mirror in bed, in a wheelchair, or when standing to look at the back of your hair when setting or combing it. Usually one side is a magnifying mirror and the other side is a regular mirror. A wing nut or similar device locks the mirror at the desired angle. You can also use the loop that fits around your neck as a stand for setting on a table or other flat surface. Check in your local department or variety stores.

Source: 16

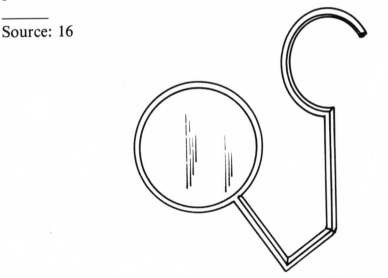

Electric-razor Holder

There is a special holder for men who have trouble using an electric razor because of limited grasp or poorly functioning fingers.

These razor holders are designed to fit three name-brand electric razors. A person who cannot grasp adequately but who does have arm function can slip his hand through the loop and use the razor without assistance. This device is made of stainless steel covered with plastic and foam padding for comfort. The loop fits around the razor and fastens with nylon looped tape to hold it securely.

Source: 20

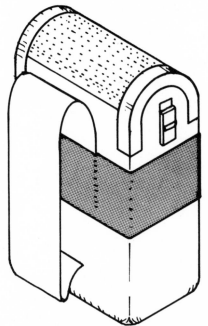

Section 4

Visual Aids

Lighted-stand Magnifier

Many persons have difficulty in reading even with fitted glasses and good light, so this lighted magnifier on a stand should be a help to some readers.

The lens and light are both adjustable. The lens is 2 inches by 4 inches, which is perhaps small for prolonged use, but it is optically ground and gives a clear sharp image from edge to edge.

When using this lighted lens, your hands are free to turn pages and adjust your reading material. The stand is chrome-plated steel and the feet are nonskid.

Source: 16

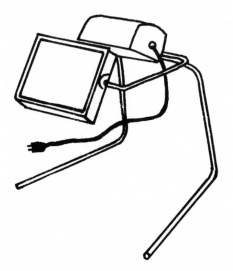

Lighted Magnifier

Problems with vision are common among readers. Performing everyday routine tasks requires some visual acuity for most of us.

This large magnifying lens is lighted and can serve many purposes around the home. The lens is 3 inches wide and the handle holds two "C" batteries, such as those used in flashlights.

Some of the uses for this lighted magnifier include reading maps, telephone books, the fine print in newspapers or magazines, or in hobbies such as stamp collecting. I have used it to search for a small item lost in the carpet. The cost is minimal so you might want to have one in your car as well as at home.

Source: 14, 16, 17

Makeshift Magnifier

If your vision is changing or failing and you find yourself without your glasses, this is a usable crutch to help read phone books, find zip codes, or determine prices.

Most of us past forty seem to have measurable changes in vision. Numbers cause a particular problem and "3," "5," and "8" seem to look alike, especially if the print is fine.

Try this! Put a small hole in a piece of paper with a pin or a sharp pencil and hold the paper to your eye, focus on the wanted number, and miraculously, it comes into view larger and sharper.

When you don't have paper, form your fist into an eyepiece. Close the other eye, forming a small hole between your palm and little finger. The small channel of light entering your eye clears the vision. I don't know exactly why it works, but it does.

Full-page Magnifier

This full-page magnifier makes it possible to view the entire page of a book or magazine at one time. The print appears four times larger than it is.

Made of unbreakable plastic, 7 inches by 10 inches, mounted in a frame, it allows you to enjoy freedom in your choice of reading material.

The biggest advantage of this full-page enlarger is that you do not have to move it to read an entire page, and this should be easier on your eyes.

Source: 13, 14

Bar Magnifier

Do you have trouble with reading the telephone book or a small-type section of the paper? This handy bar magnifier comes in a case, fits in your purse or drawer, and does a good job of enlarging type. You can readily read a phone number or the small print on a legal document. I would not recommend this for reading a book or a lengthy article. For an everyday aid I find it very helpful.

Source: 37

Sewing Machine Magnifier

We who find our eyesight deteriorating often give up the jobs we used to enjoy because they require too much effort. If you like to sew on the machine, but cannot see well enough to thread the needle, this magnifier could be a real asset.

You attach it to the side of your machine, and the magnifier swivels to just the right angle. This leaves both hands free to guide your material or thread the needle. This would also be a help in checking the size and tension of the stitch.

Source: 2

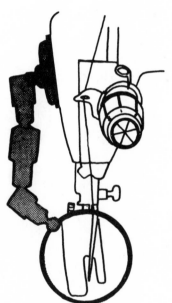

Neck Magnifier

Most women and many men enjoy doing hand-work, crewel, needlepoint, knitting, or embroidery. However, most of us suffer from gradual loss of vision and often find handwork impossible because of visual deficiencies.

This neck magnifier has helped many to continue with hobbies or handwork. The lens is 4 1/2 inches in diameter, mounted in clear lucite, and frees both hands for the work you choose to do. The lens hangs free but is braced against your chest to keep it in a steady position. You can and should continue to use your regular glasses.

Source: 13, 14, 16, 21, 28

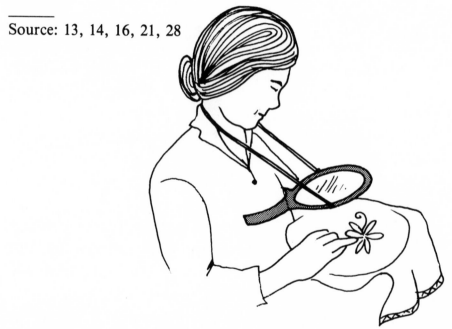

100

Insulin Syringe Magnifier

This syringe magnifier is especially designed to assist the diabetic obtain accurate measurement when administering insulin. The device clips onto the body of the syringe and magnifies the graduated scale for easy and accurate reading. It is unbreakable and is cleansed with soap and warm water. With normal usage, this should give long service.

Because impaired eyesight is often a partner to diabetes, this should fill a real need.

Source: 2, 12

Dual Night Light

Many accidents in the home can be avoided with more adequate lighting. If you get up at night, it is a good idea to have a night light to guide you. There are dozens of kinds of night lights that you can buy at hardware or variety stores. Some of them use small Christmas tree bulbs; others have neon bulbs that do not burn out.

Some lights are advertised to last forever, which should be long enough. They plug into any outlet and their light is soft, not glary. Get several—one each for the bathroom, hallway, and bedroom.

Night lights work in children's rooms to give them the sense of security they may need.

Source: 14, 17, 19, 26

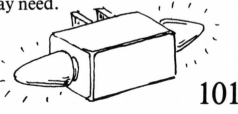

101

Bookholder

For you who are confined to bed or have weak hand and arm muscles, holding a book or magazine for any length of time is tiring or even impossible. Many bookholders are offered for sale in book or stationery stores or through mail-order catalogues.

Made of wood, plastic, or metal, this holder can be used in bed, across your lap, or placed on a table. Some have clips and a ledge on the bottom to keep the book open to the reading page. Most of them tilt for versatility. The surface is usually stain resistant. You can place the holder in a horizontal position and use it as a bed tray or for writing. For easy storage, the legs should fold flat.

Source: 14, 16, 33

Glasses Holder

Do you need your glasses to see the clock in the morning? Or maybe your visual problems demand that you wear your glasses to walk to the bathroom. My grandmother used to say, "I can't find my eyes." Her glasses were usually tucked into the high knot on top of her head.

This neat glasses case could be on your nightstand beside your bed, making your glasses easy to find, safe, and not likely to be misplaced.

The lining is felt which protects the lenses. With this case standing by your bedside, finding your "eyes" even in an emergency should be easy.

Source: 14

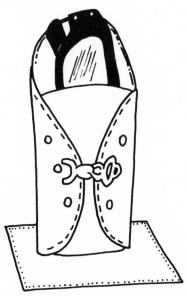

Light for Dark Corners

According to the National Safety Council, many of the home accidents could be avoided with more adequate lighting. Halls, stairways, closets, basements, and even exterior doors often do not have any kind of lighting.

An inexpensive battery operated cordless light fixture can be installed that will help solve a lighting problem when electrical outlets are not available. This operates with two "D" batteries.

Of course, this light is not adequate to read by, but it does illuminate hazards in out-of-the-way places in your home.

Source: 13, 14, 19

Make Your Own Colored Glasses

The glare from bright winter or summer sunshine is very irritating to the eyes. Some of you have dark glasses made from your prescription, but for others, an extra pair of glasses is not in the budget.

This plastic lens changes your regular glasses to darkened ones for outdoor wear. The lens wraps around the side of the eye a bit to keep the side rays from annoying you. You merely slip the lens inside your regular glasses and it hooks over the nose piece to keep firmly in place. The quality is good so your vision is not distorted. This item is available at most drugstores.

Source: 14, 26, 29

Color Tags for the Blind

Can you imagine how difficult it would be to color coordinate your clothing if you were blind? Instead of guessing or having the help of a sighted person, here is another solution—small Braille tags to be sewn into garments.

An engineer at Bell Laboratory in Murray Hill, New Jersey, created this idea. The tags are 1 inch long, 1/4 inch wide, and about the thickness of a fingernail. Stamped into the metal are symbols for 14 basic colors that enable the blind person to "read" his wardrobe. Each tag has a hole on either end to use for sewing and a small projection to indicate the top. One set consists of 56 tags.

These tags are made by the Kearney, New Jersey, chapter of Telephone Pioneers of America, a service and social organization of longtime Bell employees. These sets are distributed through the American Foundation for the Blind to the many state foundations.

Source: 2

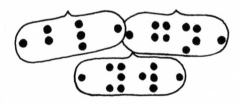

Large-type Publications

It used to be that when your vision became impaired, you had to give up reading. Public awareness has improved the lot of a large segment of our population—those with visual problems.

Large-type books, magazines, and newspapers are available at most public libraries to borrow as you borrow any other kind of book. Several monthly magazines publish a large-type edition, as do some newspapers.

Books available include the classics, old favorites, and even newer titles. The books are necessarily larger than the usual edition and the type size varies, but they are a help for you who need increased type size.

Section 5

Eating and Food Service

Scoop Plates

There are many kinds of plates especially designed to assist persons who have difficulty feeding themselves. The scoop plate looks like a fine solution to a rather common problem shared by many of our elderly and disabled citizens. A low rim in front and a high rim at the rear makes scoop-feeding easier. A rubber pad on the bottom makes the dish nonskid. You can select from many colors and the dish is dishwasher safe.

An addition that can be made to any plate in your cupboard is a steel clip-on rim. Some are partial arcs, others nearly circle the plate. Some clamp on the back of the plate, others are held on by spring action.

A variety of eating devices can be ordered through hospital supply firms, which allows you to choose one best suited to your needs.

Source: 16, 20, 33

109

Cups for Shaky Hands

For those of you with shaky or weak hands, drinking either hot or cold liquids can be dangerous as well as messy. Several solutions are pictured here. A push-button thermal mug can be used either at home or in the car. Just push the button to sip, let it go, and the mug is sealed. It will not spill even if tipped over.

You can purchase a cup with two handles which lets the weight be distributed evenly between your hands. A snorkel cup with a built-in straw can be ordered. This cup can be boiled and sterilized, is unbreakable, and will not chip.

A child's cup offers still another method. There is a hole in the removable lid that enables you to drink with no spills.

Source: 11, 13, 16, 20, 26, 33

Special Utensils

These eating dishes and utensils are especially designed for persons who have problems feeding themselves. Getting food onto a spoon or fork is difficult with the ordinary plate, so this one has a built-up edge to help push the food onto the utensil.

The cup is designed for a person with no grip. The hand slips into the open space and the cup is held by the entire hand for better balance. These dishes are made of Melamine, which is dishwasherproof and unbreakable. The silverware is stainless steel with plastic handles.

Source: 20, 27

Special Silverware

Many kinds of silverware can be purchased to solve almost any feeding problem. However, you will not find them in a regular department store. Most can be purchased through hospital supply firms or pharmacies.

Some utensils swivel to maintain a level position. Others have extra-long handles to accommodate limited arm movements. Some have extra-large built-up handles for those who cannot grasp small-sized items. You can also buy circular foam padding that will give any knife, fork, spoon, or even your toothbrush a large handle. This foam can be ordered by the yard and cut to any desired length.

Source: 16, 20, 23, 33

Knife-fork Eating Aid

This utensil is made especially for people who have the use of only one hand. The knife blade is a part of the tool and serves to cut meat or other food. The tines are then turned to pick up the bite.

The four-tined fork has a sharper edge on one side to cut food yet is not sharp enough to injure your mouth. Generally, this type of eating tool is made of stainless steel for easy cleaning and long wear.

Source: 16, 20, 27

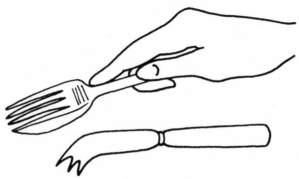

"Zipper" Orange

Peeling oranges, either by hand or with a knife, is extremely difficult for persons with weak or crippled hands. Besides, the fiber gets under your fingernails and is hard to remove.

A "zipper" orange is easily prepared with any sharp knife. Cut across the orange in slices, almost but not quite through the skin. Make one slice the opposite direction from stem end to the other end cutting only halfway through the orange. To carry in a lunch bag, wrap with plastic or place in a sandwich bag.

To eat, pull off a slice, spread it open, and the sections pop up to eat from the peel. All that is left are the slices of peeling and no mess or sticky fingers.

Section 6

Communi-
cations

Telephone Dialing Aids

Seeing accurately to dial your telephone may prevent you from ringing more than your share of wrong numbers. These two additions for your present telephone can eliminate this problem. The circular dial with enlarged numbers can be placed on your phone. It is fastened in place by a sticky back surface. Some have a glow so they may be seen in the dark.

A plastic device fits over the numbered surface of push-button phones and can be attached without tools. Persons with big or clumsy fingers, long fingernails, or impaired vision should try it.

Source: 2, 8, 20

Telephone Amplifiers

For the hard of hearing, there are several devices designed to promote better understanding of telephone conversations. Most phone companies can install special equipment on your phone. However, you can purchase some devices that are Federal Communications Commission approved to add to your present system.

A small amplifier, which you can attach yourself if your phone is the new modular type, requires no batteries. This device amplifies both your voice and that of your caller, and has a volume control switch for private adjustment. When your phone rings, you tap a small bar on the phone top, leave your phone on the hook, and talk or listen. This is a great help for a bedridden patient.

Source: 8, 20, 31

Portable Telephone Amplifier

If you have deficient hearing, this device attaches to your telephone receiver and increases the sound up to five times. It is easily attached to your phone and a snug fitting band holds it securely. The fingertip control changes the volume to suit your needs. You can carry the device in your pocket or purse to use on office or public phones.

This item is battery operated.

The telephone company can install a permanent amplifier on your home or office phone. They offer many solutions for the customer with hearing problems.

Source: 8, 31

Telephone Holder

Using the telephone may be either a business necessity or pleasurable recreation, but holding the phone is an impossibility for some.

The phone handle pictured is made of plastic-coated metal and can be bent to fit your hand size. It fastens to the receiver with VELCRO® tape. VELCRO® is a nylon two-part tape that grips securely. However, you can pull it apart easily, should you want to remove this helper.

Source: 20

Amplify Your Telephone

Most telephone companies can provide you with a special receiver that amplifies the phone conversation for you who are hard of hearing. You may also purchase a device that amplifies the sound and allows you to hear stereophonically.

You attach the gadget to the telephone, and the second receiver is held to the other ear. It can also permit a second person to listen to a conversation.

Source: 8, 34

No-hands Phone Rest

You can free your hands for taking notes or dialing the telephone by installing a shoulder rest on your present phone. This device is commonly used in offices by persons who need to make notes of telephone conversations, but it is equally useful at home and by a person who has weak or limited grasp.

The design allows the telephone to rest on either shoulder. The shoulder piece is padded with a rubber cushion for comfort.

Source: 2, 34

Special Services for Your Telephone

The Bell Telephone Company offers many solutions for those who have hearing or speech difficulties.

Special receivers to amplify sound, hearing aid adapters, headset amplifiers, and bone conduction receivers are but a few of the additions you can obtain for your home or office telephone.

Special signals can be installed to make it easier to hear the telephone ring. These include a tone ringer, a loud bell, and an 8-inch gong. One can also have a visual signal that blinks a light on and off as the bell rings. For severely handicapped patients, a speaker-phone can allow you to talk and listen without lifting the receiver.

To find a solution for your special needs, contact your local telephone office and ask for assistance.

Source: 8

Extension Speakers

Hearing deficiencies are one of the most common ailments today. Everyday activities—using the telephone, watching television, or listening to the radio—present problems to the hard of hearing, as well as to those with whom they live.

A variety of speakers can be purchased to add to your regular equipment. Several relatively inexpensive "pillow speakers" can be plugged into radio or TV and placed beside you in bed or under your pillow. Some have volume control available at your fingertips.

Another earphone speaker fits over, not in, the ear. This is really a miniature speaker and the fidelity is good. For stereophonic sound, small headphones like those used in airplanes can be added to your equipment.

Many modern radios and TVs have the built-in plug so that you may add an earphone or auxiliary speaker. If yours does not, a serviceman can install it.

Source: 31

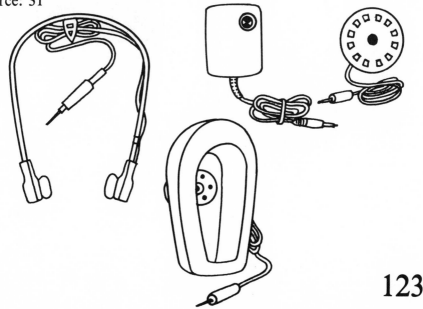

Remote Control Switch for TV or Radio

How many times have you wanted to turn off the TV or radio and had to get up from bed or a comfortable chair? A rather inexpensive extension switch can serve many uses in the home.

If you have your radio or TV adjusted to the proper station, you can turn it on or off with the flick of a finger.

This device serves as a remote control switch, but does not change the channels. Fifteen feet of cord allows flexibility. Plug the cord into the wall and the TV, radio, or stereo into the outlet in the plug. Put it by your bed or chair for instant control.

Source: 13, 14, 16, 19

Arthritic Writing Aids

Arthritics and others with grasp problems do experience great difficulty in writing with either a pen or pencil. Many devices are available.

One can be made from elastic and a few sewing stitches. Measure a piece of 1/2-inch elastic to fit around the thumb and index finger and fold to make three slots, one for the thumb, one for the finger, and one for the writing tool. Stitch or staple it to the proper size.

A wooden holder, smoothly finished and shaped to fit the palm of the hand, can be purchased. A set screw securely holds the pen or pencil in place. This tool can be guided by the shoulder, forearm, or wrist muscles.

The finger quill can be used by those who have no hand grip but can still manipulate their fingers.

Source: 16, 20, 23

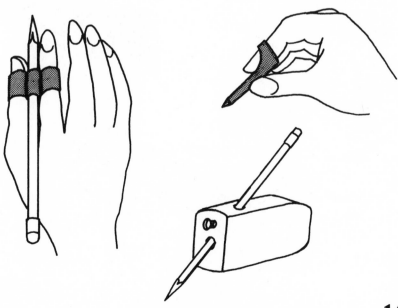

Clip Caddie or Lap Desk

For people who have the use of only one hand or who are confined to a bed or chair, a clip caddie or lap desk can help solve the problem of writing. Letters, bills, or household accounts can be kept together and handled more easily.

The clip caddie is made of simulated leather with a snap closer. The 1 1/2-inch compartment stores pens, pencils, paper, stamps, checkbook—even bills. The clip at the top steadies the paper.

The lap desk is made of pine with a slanted top that lifts. The interior may also be used to store stationery supplies.

Sources:
Clip caddie 16
Desk 12, 14

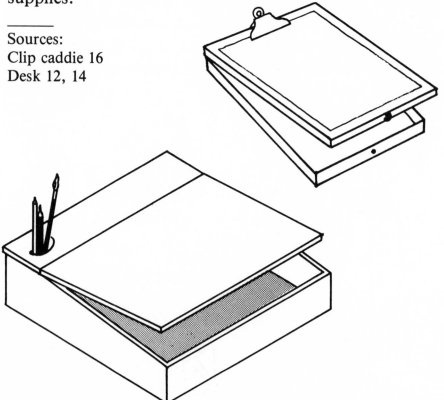

How-to for the Left-handed

When I was young it was fun to try to write left-handed, but the results were never very successful. If for some reason you have to become a "leftie," here is help for you.

A 30-page manual of instructions to teach you to write with your left hand can be purchased. Included are exercises with illustrations for learning, improving, or converting to left-handed writing.

A one-handed writing board equipped with small rubber feet to keep the board from "walking" can be ordered from the same source. This item can be converted to either right- or left-handed use.

Source: 20

Left-handed Stationery Supplies

There is great news for all of you "lefties." I know being left-handed isn't exactly a handicap, but our world is programmed for the right-handed. Many of our everyday utensils are impossible to use with the left hand, such as scissors, paring knives, notebooks, playing cards, can openers, vegetable peelers, irons, golf gloves, and corkscrews.

Special pens for lettering and writing italics are made for left-handed persons. Left-handed notebooks with the spiral binding on the right, a left-handed address book, and a memo board with the pen on the left are all available.

Included also are instructions for left-handed knitting, crocheting, and other crafts.

Source: 20, 27

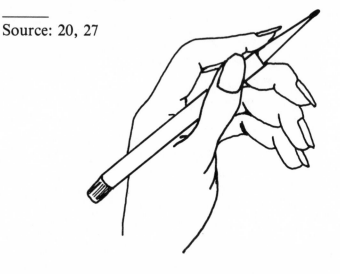

Section 7

Wheelchair Specials

Transfer Board

We visited a relative who is confined to a wheel-chair. His desire is to be as independent as possible. He uses a transfer board to get from his wheelchair to his car or his bed. I have never seen anyone so adept at moving around with no help from others.

This maple transfer board has tapered ends to allow you to slide on or off easily. You can attach a rope handle that gives you a place to grasp for placing the board where you need it. Some come with a small hole in the board for this same purpose. The size and price varies with suppliers.

Source: 16, 20, 29

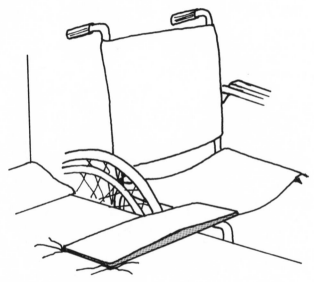

Lap Tray for Wheelchair

When you spend most of your time in a wheelchair, you know some of your special needs. For you to eat or work at a table or desk, your chair must be the right height to roll under the table top.

A practical alternative is a lap tray. These trays come in various materials and sizes. Some are clear plastic that is nearly invisible and lets you see your way around the house more easily. Other models are made of Formica or Masonite. All models are fastened onto the arms of the chair to prevent slipping or tipping.

Lap boards enable a wheelchair patient to write, eat, sew, or do handwork or crafts with ease and comfort.

Source: 16, 20, 29, 33

Footplate Carpet

Spending your waking hours in a wheelchair creates many unique problems. The steel footplate on a wheelchair can be very damaging to a patient's legs, ankles, and feet—causing lacerations that may require medical attention. The footplate also creates hazards for the nursing personnel or attendants who happen to bump into it.

This "slipcover" for the footplate consists of a piece of carpeting with a backing so that it slips over the footplate and is held firmly in place.

Besides the protection this offers, it is also warmer and more comfortable for the patient's feet. You could made these covers from carpet scraps, or you can buy them ready-made.

Source: 20, 29

Wheelchair Carryalls

For those of you in wheelchairs, here are two suggestions for carryalls to hold the many things you need to have near you.

This cloth bag, made of heavy denim, has several pockets to carry your glasses, handkerchief, coin purse, or writing equipment. You fasten it over the arm of the chair and it is held securely with some type of fastener.

A small narrow knitting bag also serves this purpose. This should have a full-length zipper for convenience. Because it is narrow, you can slip it between you and the chair arm.

Source: 16, 20, 33, 39

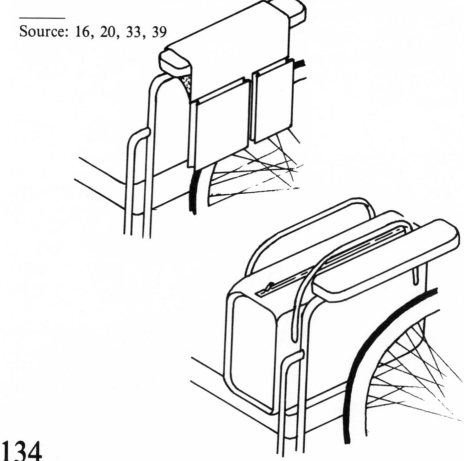

134

Wheelchair Alternative

Many people who must sit to work have suggested alternatives to a regular wheelchair. A roll-about secretary's chair can be used. The casters move easily and if patients can use their feet to propel their chairs, they can get around their houses comfortably and continue their daily routine tasks.

Many other models, all equipped with easy rolling wheels, can be found in hospital supply catalogues. Some are made of vinyl for easy cleaning and others use webbing or heavy plastic.

A push bar behind the chairback allows another person to push the patient. Some models have a tilt footrest that can be folded back out of the way. Select carefully the model that will fit your needs most adequately.

Source: 16, 29, 33

Telescoping Magnet

This telescoping magnet is a great idea for those confined to wheelchairs or who cannot bend over or stoop down.

This magnet fits in your pocket much like a fountain pen with a clip. It is 5 inches long and extends to 19 inches. You can pick up any items made of steel and the magnet is strong enough to attract and hold eating utensils. It is rustproof and chrome-plated. This gadget will save you from lots of stooping and bending.

Source: 16

Door Openers and Closers

In a wheelchair it is difficult to close a door after yourself. You are too far away from the doorknob, and the wheelchair is in the way.

Two devices pictured here help solve this problem. One is merely a long leather thong fastened to the doorknob. An invalid friend suggested fastening some small bells to the thongs, which make a pleasant jingle when the door is opened or closed.

The other device can be homemade from a large dowel pin or a broom handle. Fasten a leather loop on one end and install a cane tip on the other. The loop serves as the door shutter when you hook it around the doorknob. Hang it on a hook near the door for the next use.

Source: 23

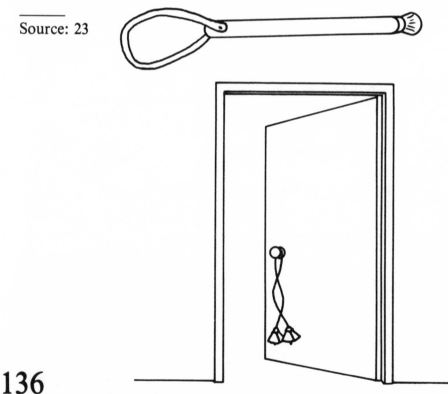

Wheelchair Caddy

Some people are confined to wheelchairs all their waking hours. Arthritics, stroke victims, amputees, and paraplegics are but a few of those who would find this wheelchair caddy a welcome assistance in their daily routines.

The caddy fastens on the arm of the wheelchair and is used to keep your personal belongings at your fingertips. There are several compartments, with spaces for magazines, newspapers, coffee cup or drinking glass, spectacles, coin purse, cleansing tissues, or medicines.

This accessory is designed to mount on any kind of wheelchair, including those with fixed arms, detachable arms, and detachable desk arms. It is lightweight, easy to install, made of plastic, and washable.

Source: 29

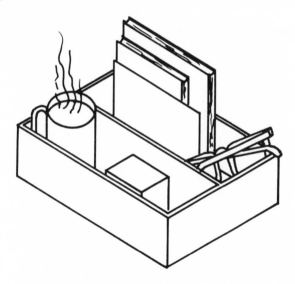

Short-handled Cleaning Equipment

We all know that dust and dirt collect on tiles or linoleum floors. Trying to manage a long-handled broom and a small dustpan is impossible for people in wheelchairs.

Try a short-handled broom and a long-handled dustpan. The shorter broom is often narrower than conventional types but is still efficient. The long-handled dustpan makes it possible for anyone to sweep up debris without stooping. This should help those who have back trouble.

A large loop of strap leather can be fastened to the side of the broom handle or other cleaning tool. An almost useless arm or an arm stump can be slipped into the loop. This should prevent dropping the broom.

Source: 16

Section 8

Relieving Aches

Bed Board

A backache can make you uncomfortable all over. Some of the backache problems can be relieved by improving the bed on which you sleep. However, not everyone can afford to buy a new firm mattress and/or springs; so this less expensive solution may prove helpful.

Use a bed board. This can be a piece of plywood long enough to reach at least from your shoulders to your knees. Place it between the springs and the mattress and this helps to eliminate the sag that causes discomfort.

You can purchase a folding bed board that is portable, and you can even carry it with you to use in a hotel or motel. Of course, there is no need to remove this board from your bed unless you change sleeping quarters.

Source: 28, 29

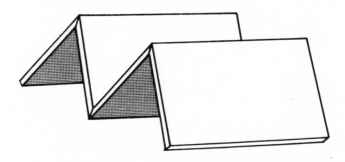

Backache Relief

An orthopedic surgeon told me that the most common complaint from his patients was lower back pain. The causes are many and I know nothing about cures. However, this cushion does offer some relief from the pain and discomfort.

This curved cushion was designed by an orthopedic specialist and can be used wherever you sit—at home, driving or riding, watching TV, or at the office. The unique design relieves tension and pressure on the spine. It would be wise to consult your physician before purchasing the pillow.

The pad is made of solid urethane and comes equipped with a removable, washable cover.

Source: 13, 14, 16, 17, 26

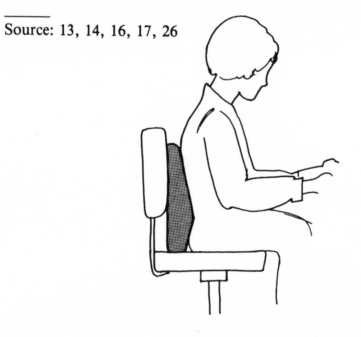

Save Your Hands

Arthritis is rightfully called the "great crippler," and as the disease progresses, getting out of bed or up from a chair can become increasingly difficult.

This suggestion was given to me by a hospital therapist. Do not use your fingers to help lift your body weight from a sitting position. By turning your hand, you can use the palm which allows your body weight to be supported through your wrist instead of the fingers.

I realize that each patient is different and this might not work for everyone, but you may find it helpful.

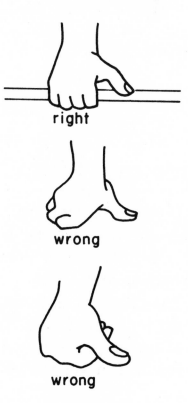

right

wrong

wrong

143

Skin Protectors

Heels and elbows are especially sensitive to irritation when you spend time in bed, as many invalids have to do. Protectors made of soft resilient Kodel polyester fiber serve to alleviate this problem. They are sold in pairs for either heels or elbows and fasten with VELCRO® to keep them in place.

These protectors are ventilated to prevent overheating and excessive perspiration. You can also purchase a larger size protector for the entire foot.

The outer surface slides over the sheets easily, and they are machine washable.

Source: 16, 33

Knee-rest Pillow

If you suffer from back trouble, you often find that lying with your legs flat is most uncomfortable. This wide triangular-shaped pillow helps to relieve the pain in both back and legs.

The pillow is made of foam and has a cover that zips off for laundry care. This solution is better than a pile of ordinary pillows that slip and slide and do not give you the firm support you need.

Source: 14

Inflatable Pillow

When you have to sit for a long period of time, you become uncomfortable and a change is a welcome relief. An inflatable pillow can provide a comfortable sitting surface, especially if you are inclined to be thin or bony.

This pillow is made of vinyl and each side inflates separately for maximum comfort and adjustability. When deflated, the pillow will fit in a pocket or purse. Because it is air filled and lightweight, the pillow can be transferred from chair to chair or to an automobile.

Source: 16

Flotation Pillow

Persons with disabilities or muscle weaknesses have to sit a great deal of the time and may find this flotation pillow a comfortable addition to either a wheelchair or a regular chair.

The pillow is made of polyurethane foam covered with black vinyl. A valve allows the user to fill it with water, which helps distribute the body weight and relieve irritations caused by harder surfaces. When inflated, the pillow measures 16 inches by 16 inches by 1 1/4 inches. You can clean it easily with a damp cloth.

Source: 33

Arm Cushion

This arm cushion can be used to relieve the strain and pain common to arthritic or mastectomy patients.

The sore, sensitive arm is cradled in the shaped vinyl cushion. The shoulder is slightly arched and the elbow, wrist, and fingers relax.

You can adjust for softness and height. A zippered cover permits easy laundering. Extra covers may be ordered.

Source: 16

Tubular Bandage and Corn Pads

Trying to keep a bandage on a sore finger or toe can be frustrating. This tubular bandage fits all toes and fingers securely. Made of soft foam and lined with cotton, it protects cuts, bruises, corns, blisters, and bunions. You will find this easy to use. Just cut off the desired length and slip it over the injury. The large size fits adults; the small size is for children, little fingers, and toes. It comes in a 36-inch roll.

The corn pads come in a set of three, in sizes small, medium, and large. This item can be used on corns, hammer toes, and ingrown nails. The pads are washable and nonallergenic.

Source: (1) 14, 26; (2) 16

Footbath Massager

You have heard it said that when your feet hurt, you hurt all over. This is true.

Causes of foot pain are varied and many, from arthritis and gout to tight shoes or corns. Many of you I'm sure have soaked your tired aching feet in warm water to relieve the pain.

An electric vibrating bath helps to relieve foot discomfort. This tub is 17 inches by 14 inches by 6 inches, with a powerful motor that vibrates and circulates the water and soothes tired or swollen feet. This vibrating bath can also be used for hands, arms, or elbows.

The motor is UL approved, and the tub is made of sturdy plastic for long life.

These baths are available from medical supply firms, some pharmacies, and from mail-order catalogues. The prices vary.

Source: 33

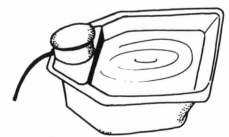

Moist Heating Pad

For aches and pains of arthritis and other similar ailments, doctors usually prescribe moist heat. This can mean wetting and wringing out towels with hot water or tying with a bandage or plastic wrap. It is generally a messy job.

Why not use a moist heating pad? There are many on the market and they are usually available in pharmacies.

A man-made sponge is moistened, slipped into a pocket next to the heating pad, and placed on the aching muscle. The heat from the pad keeps the sponge warm, and it stays damp for a surprisingly long time. You can remove the sponge and use the heating pad dry.

The switch should be adjustable, the cord and heating pad should both have the UL seal of approval, and a terry cloth cover will permit easy washing.

Source: 13, 16, 29, 33

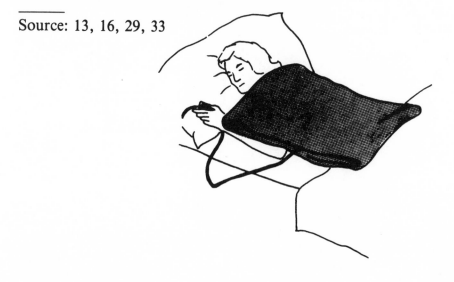

Massage Heating Pad

When you have a backache, nothing feels better or relaxes you more than heat and massage. This vinyl covered flexible body massager with heat is a pleasure to use.

The design allows you to use this pad on any part of your body. VELCRO® fasteners help to hold it in place on your back or leg or ankle.

The massage action is built-in and the switch offers heat alone, massage alone, or both heat and massage. It is small enough to carry in a suitcase. The pad is UL approved and uses only 50 watts. Relax and enjoy it!

Source: 19, 29, 33

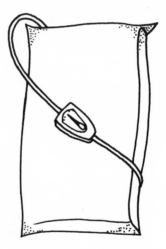

Flexible Heating Pad

A relatively new item on the market is a flexible heating pad. This fits snuggly against most any part of the body and can be fastened in place with a tie or straps of VELCRO.®

This wrapped pad would solve the problem of applying heat to the lower back, an area that causes many people discomfort. Because of its flexibility, the pad hugs the body to give welcome relief from many kinds of aches and pains. The Underwriters seal of approval guarantees your safety.

Source: 29, 36

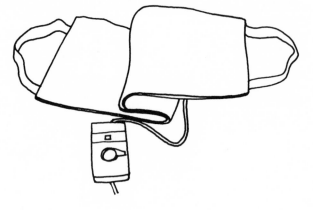

Heated Mitt for Aching Joints

According to my arthritic friends, keeping the fingers flexible is a painful problem. Heat does add a measure of comfort to the afflicted joints.

This roll-up heating pad, 8 1/2 inches by 3 1/2 inches by 12 inches long, can soothe hands, elbows, knees, feet, and ankles. The muff can be used either with moist or dry heat and is roomy enough to exercise your fingers or toes while enjoying the warmth.

This heating pad is UL approved, and guaranteed for two years. The cover is removable and washable. Three heat settings, knitted cuffs, and VELCRO® closure add to the versatility of this appliance.

Source: 11, 29, 33

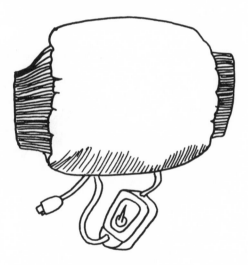

Fitted Heating Pad

Pain in knee and elbow joints is a common complaint of arthritics and those who suffer from similar ailments. This knee-elbow heating pad is fitted to provide soothing warmth where it is needed. It is cupped to fit the elbow, shoulder, or knee and is fastened with a strap closure made of VELCRO.®

The thermostat has three heat settings and a pilot light to indicate the appliance is "on." The cover is washable.

The UL seal of approval assures you of its safety. The heavy-duty cord is 7 feet long. Using only 40 watts of power, the operating cost is minimal.

Source: 11, 16

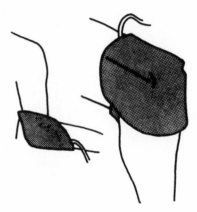

Section 9

Sewing and Handwork

Needle Threader

Sewing can be fun, but it is frustrating to try to thread a needle when your eyes are weak or your hands are a bit shaky. Many kinds of gadgets are on the market, but this one pictured works easily.

The needle is inserted eye-down into the hole, the thread is placed in a groove, you press a button, and the needle is threaded. A sharp blade on the side serves as a thread cutter.

At some fabric stores you can buy self-threading needles for both hand and machine sewing. You might try these, but the thread must be quite strong so that it does not break under stress.

Source: 2, 16, 20

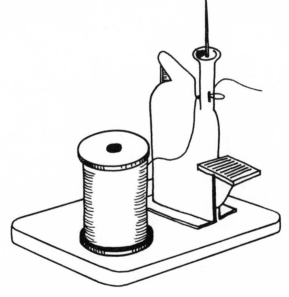

Easy-thread Needle

With advancing years, the needle eyes seem to get smaller or at least many of us have trouble threading a needle. This needle eye expands almost the length of the needle and then snaps back into place for sewing.

This should help those of you with arthritis, palsy, or visual impairment. The needle is relatively fine, made of steel, and gold finished. You can easily find it in your pincushion.

A package of these needles would make a nice gift for someone who still likes to sew.

Source: 2, 11, 26

Left-handed Scissors

Most everything from wristwatches to scissors are awkward for the left-handed person. Some of you have learned to cope and use the right-handed versions.

Left-handed scissors come in all styles and sizes from children's blunt point to kitchen snippers to fine dressmaking shears.

With left-handed scissors, you can see the cutting line clearly because of the blade alignment. No longer do you have to be a contortionist.

Source: 15, 19, 20, 21, 27

Clamp Embroidery Hoop

A clamp-on embroidery hoop would be a real asset to a person with the use of only one hand who still wants to do handwork. Normal use of a hoop requires both hands and considerable effort. This clamp fits tightly on a table, chair, or lapboard. It won't mar the surface, is nonrust, nonslip, and swivels. The hoop can be adjusted up or down and tilts to any position.

The material is polished hardwood. You can order either an 8- or 10-inch hoop and continue to enjoy needlework with a minimum of effort.

Source: 16

Sit-on Needlework Frame

If you like to do needlepoint, crewel embroidery, or other types of handwork, a frame that you sit on could be a fine addition to your sewing department.

This frame can be adjusted for either right- or left-hand use and is designed to hold the material taut and smooth. It is also adjustable in both height and angle to help the worker be most comfortable.

Similar items also come with large, round, fit-together hoops. By sitting on the support, both hands are free to do the handwork.

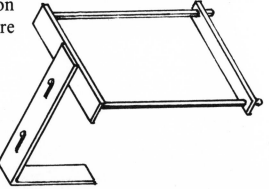

Source: 21

Easy-wear Apron

Many of us still like to wear an apron to protect our clothing when doing kitchen or housework. Tying a bow or a knot is very difficult for a person who has hand problems. For a homemaker who is one-handed or cannot tie a bow, an apron hoop can solve the problem.

This flexible plastic hoop can be used with any kind of material. Cut a piece 6 inches wide the entire length of the fabric (this makes pockets). Hem one side of this strip. With the right side of pocket piece against the wrong side of the main apron, seam the bottom and side. Hem the edges to the top. Make a 2-inch hem at the top of the apron. Insert the loop in the top hem. You can separate the pocket into compartments with a single or double row of stitching. These pockets can be used to carry your cleaning materials or to serve as a depository for "pickups."

The apron slides off the hoop for easy laundering.

Source for hoops: 16, 20, 21

Section 10

Moving About

Walker with Seat

You all know persons who use a walker because they are unsteady when walking or are recovering from some surgery or accident. A walker designed especially for those who are unable to walk very far without resting is available. This unique walker has a fold-down seat made of heavy canvas duck. It can be raised or lowered from either side with one hand. The seat height is 24 inches, which is comfortable, yet easy to arise from.

The lightweight, sturdy aluminum frame, rubber-tipped legs for safety, and handgrips for easy holding make this walker especially suited to persons with specific problems. Some models have adjustable legs for either a short or tall person.

Source: 29, 40

Carryall Walker Basket

Many of you probably use walkers for better mobility. A walker does assist with the chore of walking, but it usually requires both hands to manipulate adequately. Carrying anything from place to place is a critical problem.

A carryall basket made of cloth or plastic can be ordered by mail. This attaches to the crossbar of the walker, has pockets to hold household items, and frees the hands to manipulate the walker safely.

Another basket attaches to the walker and holds larger and bulkier items.The basket made of plastic-coated wire fits between the vertical legs of the walker and stays balanced in a horizontal position when in use.

Source: 29, 39

Cane Seat

Do you ever get tired while standing in line? Most people do. This strolling seat cane opens easily and makes a comfortable resting place while you wait. You don't have to be elderly or infirm to enjoy this device.

The cane is made of aluminum, weighs less than two pounds, and has firm tripod legs for extra security. The legs are rubber tipped for indoor and outdoor use. When you stop to rest, chat, or have refreshments you can just flip this cane and have a secure nontipping seat. Take it to the fair, a parade, the airport, or on a shopping trip.

Source: 14, 16, 26

Half-step

Steps can be the worst obstacle that a severely handicapped person has to cope with in the daily routine of living. The ideal solution would be to eliminate all steps in the environment; since that is rarely possible, other solutions become necessary.

Wherever possible, ramps should replace two or three high steps, but ramps of the proper slope take considerably more space than steps. A portable half-step can be made and used effectively if there is a railing beside the flight of stairs.

The half-step should fit onto the step without overhanging and should be wide enough for both feet to stand on. The handle should be long enough for the user to reach when standing on the step above. The usual riser is 7 inches, so the half-step should measure 3 1/2- inches high.

To use a half-step, place one foot on the half-step, the other foot on the next step, lift the half-step to this step, and proceed.

Source: 23 (directions for making)

Cane or Crutch Parker

Where can you put your cane while seated at a table or desk? This cane or crutch parker snaps onto your cane or crutch and slides easily under the edge of tables, counters, desk tops, or chair arms—anywhere there is a flat horizontal surface.

When there is no available area under a counter top or table, you can hang the cane over the table or desk top. For extra security with heavy crutches, two parkers can be used, one under and one over the surface.

This item is purchased by size: 3/4 inch, 7/8 inch, or one inch in diameter. Order according to the size of your cane.

Source: 20

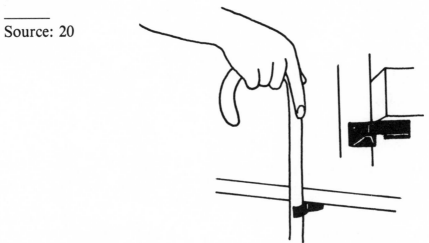

Ice Cane for Winter

In winter many of you are plagued by the fear of going outdoors because you may fall on the snow or ice. This ice cane comes recommended from a firm in Vermont.

The four sharp, steel harpoon tongs support any weight and give you a feeling of assurance while either walking or standing on slippery walks or driveways. The main part of the cane is made of heavy steel tubing.

For extra security, some shoe spikes would be a help.

Source: 17, 37

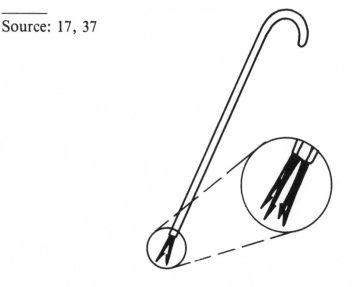

Shoe Spikes for Ice

In many areas of this country, the winter snow and ice make the roads, sidewalks, steps, and driveways slick and dangerous. The icy conditions are hazardous for everyone but frightening for you who are a bit unsteady.

Many kinds of safety shoe spikes are available from mail-order firms and shoe-repair shops. Some are much better than others and the price varies from $2 to $15.

These pictured have steel cleats imbedded in high quality rubber. You slip them over your shoe or regular rubber. You can fit them in your pocket or purse because they fold into a neat package. You buy them by the size of your regular shoe.

Source: 14, 37

Purse for Crutch

I don't have to remind crutch users how difficult it is to walk and try to carry anything. This bag, to be carried on a crutch, is designed with you in mind.

The bag is made of fabric and vinyl. You can hook it onto the crutch and it serves as a purse for a shopping trip or a carryall around the home.

The bag comes in various color combinations such as black/tan, brown/beige, oyster/beige, and light blue/navy.

Source: 39

Door Opener

Limited grasp, weak muscles, or crippled hands can make it nearly impossible to open a door fitted with the usual round slippery handle. You can replace the entire handle and latch with a lever-type handle, but some other solutions are illustrated.

Several types of attachments can be purchased that permit easy door opening. If a keyhole is in the knob itself, it is still accessible. You can also mount this device for hip action opening.

Source: 16, 20

Key Holder for Weak Hands

If you have trouble with finger function, you no doubt have trouble using a key, either in a door or an automobile.

Any key can be built up with wood to provide a firm usable handle. This one is fastened onto the key with a bolt and wing nut. A small dowel pin is inserted through the wood to make turning the key an easy task.

This type of handle can be made in any size to fit the need of the user. A ring can be attached to allow you to hang the key.

Source: 20, 23, 33

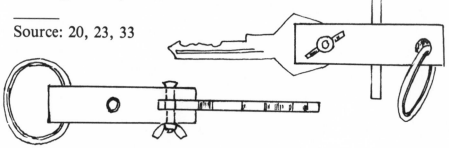

Car Door Opener

Opening a car door can be tricky for people with normal grasp and strength, but for an arthritic or a stroke victim, it is often impossible.

This aid pictured was designed to open push-button doors. It can also open seat belts. Used as a lever, it will open every type of handle both inside and outside a car.

Source: 23

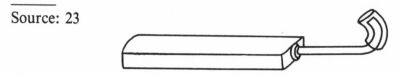

For Women Only

Reach to Recovery

A program sponsored by the American Cancer Society, called Reach to Recovery, is available in most areas of this country. The program was started in 1953 by Teresa Lasser, widow of J. K. Lasser (the author of many income tax guides). The American Cancer Society adopted this program as part of their rehabilitation program in 1963.

Hundreds of women throughout the United States are volunteers in this program. These women have all had mastectomies. They receive training by other volunteers so that they may call on patients who have had similar surgery. The patient's doctor must request the visit through the local coordinator for Reach to Recovery. She in turn calls a volunteer who visits the patient, usually while she is still in the hospital.

The helpful call from another woman who has had similar surgery is encouraging to the patient psychologically, physically, and cosmetically. Besides giving her encouragement, the visitor also gives the patient a temporary breast form, shows a few simple exercises if the doctor prescribes this, and some literature for her and her family to read at leisure.

With proper exercise and a desire to be active again, most patients resume their regular routines and participate in active sports, if they choose to, within a relatively short time.

Source: 3

Prosthesis for Mastectomy Patients

The types of prostheses available include many styles and the choice is a personal matter to be decided by the patient. Some breast forms are weighted and this type is especially comfortable for a full-busted woman. Others can be filled with air, air and liquid, air and fluid, foam, foam rubber, or sterilized seed.

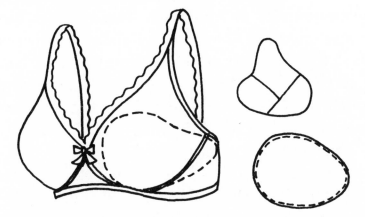

Liquid-filled forms and those containing silicone gel are somewhat more expensive, but may be exactly what you need to achieve the natural look. The important thing is to try to purchase a form that as nearly as possible duplicates the size and shape of the other breast. A bit of shopping and experimenting may be necessary to find a solution.

Special bras are available that have pockets to hold the form and keep it from slipping. Some bras have extra-wide elastic around the chest that helps keep the bra in place. Many prostheses are usable in regular bras. Then you can use the garments you have. The American

Cancer Society has a pattern for a breast form that may be made at home and filled with weighted material such as bird seed, rice, barley, or small plastic beads.

With a well-fitting breast form, you can look great in your clothes—the way you always did—and have the confidence and feeling of security that comes with having a balanced figure.

Source: 5, 10, 25, 28, 29, 32, 33

Special Swimsuits

Women who have had a radical mastectomy have special problems finding a swimsuit that hides the operation and is flattering to them. The bare shoulder, halter neckline, and bra tops are neither comfortable nor becoming.

Many swimsuit manufacturers have designed suits with higher than usual necklines, small cap sleeves, and even long sleeves, with the requirements of these women in mind. Some shops will special-order such a suit for you, but they are rarely a part of the regular stock.

One company carries a wide variety of beachwear and the prices are comparable to those in any department store. Some have matching cover-ups or skirts.

Source: 9

Section 12

Keeping Warm

Draft Stopper

With winter comes the cold and wind, which can be a bone-chilling problem if your home does not have tight windows and doors.

An idea that originated in New England and was improved upon recently to include thermal insulation, is the draft guard. This all-cotton, 43-inch-long, weighted guard will stay in place at either door or window and keeps the drafts from cooling your home. When not in use, hang it over the doorknob.

Source: 13, 14, 17, 26, 34, 35, 37, 38

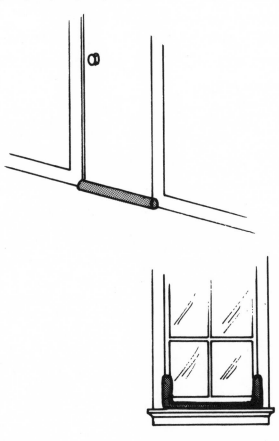

Electric Foot Warmer

Sometimes it seems to take hours to warm your feet after you've been out in the winter weather. Poor circulation and other ailments can contribute to this discomfort too.

This cushiony toaster works like a heating pad. It is roomy in size, 12 inches by 14 inches by 6 inches high, which allows plenty of toe room, and fits any foot size. Both your feet are partially enclosed.

You can use this heater in bed, on the floor, on a footstool, or on the footrests of a wheelchair. The covering is made from attractive upholstery material that is strong enough to give longtime service.

The warmth, pleasant to those who work outside as well as to those who have poor circulation, is soothing to aches and pains.

Source: 11, 35

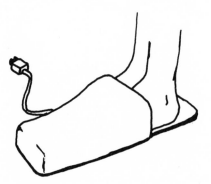

Insulated Socks

Are your feet cold all of the time? Indoors and out-doors?

These insulated socks will help. They are made of quilted nylon and are filled with insulating dacron. You can wash them in the machine and they will not shrink.

These can be worn as slippers or inside your boots or shoes for cozy warmth. They would be a useful gift for someone in a wheelchair.

These socks are ordered by size: small, medium, large, or extra large.

Another similar bootie is filled with goose down. They are also washable and warm. One size fits all.

Source: 14, 26, 34

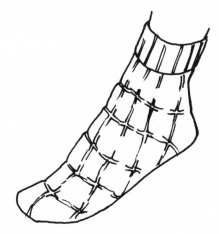

Nonelectric Heating Pads

If you have aching joints and do not choose to sit with a heating pad on the site of the pain, these unique warmers may help.

Five different sizes or shapes to fit shoulders, backs, hands, or knees give you a selection to try. These pads capture and concentrate your body's natural heat and help to transmit this heat to the affected joint.

They are foam lined and thin, and you can wear them under your regular clothing.

Source: 18, 26

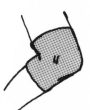

Chest Warmer

For those of you who have to be outside in the cold of winter, this chest warmer will keep you snug and warm. It is quilted nylon, filled with goose down, and gives extra protection around the chest and neck where jackets and sweaters do not provide enough warmth.

Goose down is a lightweight but superwarm insulating material. The turtleneck is ribbed in stretch knit to slip over your head easily.

Another similar chest warmer is filled with dacron and is a bit less expensive.

———

Source: 6, 7, 34

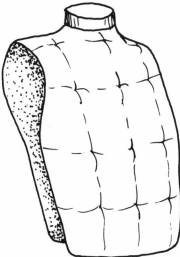

Knee Warmers

When winter strikes, keeping warm is an acute problem for the aging or for one in a wheelchair. Those of you who suffer from arthritis know about knee pains, but these wool or synthetic knee warmers can help solve the problem.

The warmers are 12 inches long, and come in small, medium, large, or extra-large sizes. If wool is irritating to you, get those made of acrylic yarn. Slip them on either under or over your stockings and feel comfortable even when your house is cool.

Source: 16, 17, 26, 33, 34, 37

Wool and Cotton Hose

Cold weather and a drafty house increases the discomfort that many of you experience. When you are relatively inactive, your legs and feet and knees are cold.

Flesh-colored wool hose can be worn under your regular nylons. They can also be worn as regular hose because they are not heavy looking.

Another kind of stocking is made of cotton lisle. These are especially beneficial for those who may be allergic to nylon. Of course, these hose are NOT panty hose so they must be worn with garters of some kind.

Source: 16, 17, 28, 35, 37

Section 13

Resting and Sleep

Makeshift Bed Rest

Being confined to bed for even a limited time can be very tiring and often makes the back ache. However, a change in position can keep a person from becoming too tired and from developing bed sores. Try this makeshift backrest.

Place a straight chair (like you use at a table or desk) at the head of the bed, upside down. The back and legs of the chair make a slanted surface against which you can prop a pillow or two.

This allows the bed patient to sit up for a time, change position, change the stress points of the body, and solves a temporary problem.

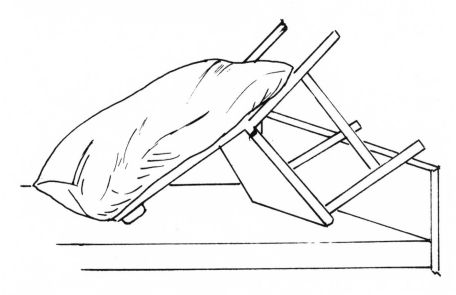

Canvas-covered Backrest

For readers who must spend much of their time in bed, this backrest is made for you. It gives firm support for sitting comfort while reading, writing, or watching TV in bed. The angle is adjustable from upright to a 20-degree incline. The back locks securely so it won't move, and your body weight keeps the device from slipping.

The frame is chromium and is tall enough to support your head and shoulders. An elastic strap holds a pillow in place. The cotton canvas cover is removable for washing and the wooden arms swing out of the way if desired. It can be folded flat for easy storage.

Source: 16

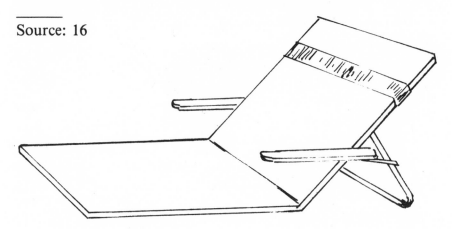

Sleeping Mask

Some of you need to take daytime rests but find it difficult to sleep because light bothers you. This black sleep mask blocks out the light and allows you a more restful sleep. It also works if your sleeping partner reads during the night and has a light turned on that disturbs you.

The mask is made of black rayon and is fastened around your head with an elastic band that holds it firmly but not too tightly. A soft cushioning on the inner side makes it comfortable and nonirritating.

Source: 14

Wedge-shaped Pillow

This wedge-shaped pillow can be used to elevate either your head or feet. If you have trouble breathing when lying down, or have back or neck problems, this sloping pillow should be a big help. It is also useful for those of you who are more comfortable with your legs elevated.

The pillow is made of foam and supports the body from the waist to the head. It has a zip-off cover that is washable. The size is approximately 24 inches by 27 inches by 6 1/2 inches.

Source: 14, 26, 28

Raise Bed with Wooden Blocks

When you experience trouble getting in or out of bed, consider lifting the bed on solid wooden blocks. These can be purchased at a lumber yard and can be hollowed out enough to hold the bed legs. They will raise the height of your bed any number of inches. This is especially helpful when you have stiff legs or lack strength to raise your body from a sitting position.

For a person who is bedridden and will be for a long time, buying a hospital-type bed would be a more satisfactory solution.

Chair Leg Elevators

Many persons find that ordinary chairs in a home are too low to use comfortably when their own legs are weak and muscle strength is deficient. Try to make the chair higher.

These strong steel brackets clamp to the bottom of either round or square legs. They are usable on either chairs or tables and extend from 3 to 7 inches. You can buy them in sets of four. These extenders fit square legs up to 1 inch across and round legs up to 1 1/4 inches in diameter.

When a chair is higher, you use less effort to rise to a standing position.

Source: 20

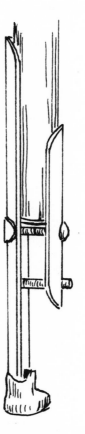

Blanket Support

Those who suffer from arthritis or other ailments of the legs and feet know that the weight of even the lightest blanket can be irritating. A blanket support that fits on the end of the bed may be the solution to a good, comfortable, and sound sleep. This device fits all beds and lifts any kind of covers (regular or contoured) off your feet for a more restful sleep.

The support folds invisibly flat when not in use. The extended base and wings form a shelf to hold the spread or blankets within comfortable reach of the person in bed.

Source: 16, 17, 26, 33

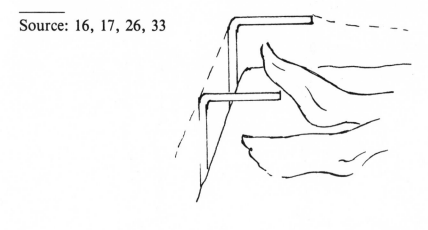

190

Section 14

Miscellaneous

Lifesaving Medical Tags

An emergency medical identification tag can be a real lifesaver for those of you who have a severe allergy or some physical ailment that requires special attention. Emergency personnel, such as ambulance attendants, police, or patrolmen, are all trained to take note of an emergency tag that an accident victim wears on his watchband, neck chain or bracelet.

The tag, made of noncorrosive metal, contains your name, address, phone number, and instructions concerning your particular problem. You can include blood type and Rh factor.

Some common concerns include allergies to sulfa, penicillin, horse serum, bee stings, and codeine. You should include information about your status as a diabetic, asthmatic, epileptic, contact lens wearer, or heart, multiple sclerosis, or hemophilia patient.

Order the tag of your choice at your local pharmacy.

Source: 29

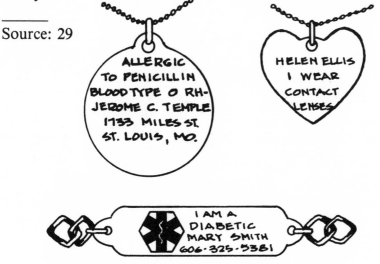

Built-up Light Switch

Turning on some light switches can be frustrating, if not impossible, if you have limited grasp.

This 4-spoked, large-sized handle fits on the switch with screw-type threads. This gives enough leverage for even the weakest hands to turn on the light. This device is made from plastic and fits on most standard lamps.

A clever person could probably carve one from lightweight wood and use a quality glue to install it. However, the price is reasonable.

Source: 20

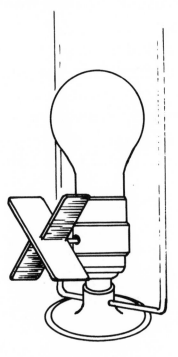

On-Off Switch

Another solution to the problem of tiny switches on lamps can be purchased at your local hardware store and installed easily into the lamp cord.

Called a line switch, it is wired into the cord and gives you positive on-off control without reaching for the regular switch.

Place the switch in a convenient location on the cord. You can arrange to have the control almost at your fingertips for a bedside lamp.

For electric appliances that do not have an on-off switch, this same device can be used. Be sure however, that you purchase a switch of adequate size to handle the wattage of the appliance.

Source: 19

Easy Switch Control

Some switches on lamps and appliances are very difficult to turn when fingers are weak or wrist action is impaired. This handy at-the-wall control for lamps, appliances, and tools should help those who have hand problems.

You plug the control into the wall outlet, and the lamp or appliance is plugged into the opposite side of the switch. A positive off-on toggle on the top enables the user to control the flow of current with ease.

Rated at 15 amperes, this switch should accommodate most small household appliances or lamps.

Source: 16

Shorten Electrical Cords

Statistics show that a large number of accidents occur in the home. Many of these can be prevented with proper planning, storage, and an extra measure of care.

For instance, light cords, TV cords, and similar connections we use on electrical appliances and lamps are often too long for the distance from the electrical outlet. This gadget will help.

You can shorten any electrical cord so that only the needed length is left. The cords look neat and are protected and kept tangle free.

Source: 14, 19

THIS...

NOT THIS

Wedge Alarm for Doors

Here is an inexpensive alarm to warn you of intruders who may try to enter your home. This wedge-shaped device blocks entry and releases a loud alarm if someone tries to open the door. Of course, the alarm may frighten you, too, but the intent is to scare the would-be burglar. It would alert you to notify the police, if necessary.

This alarm is operated with small batteries and is compact enough to carry with you on trips to use on motel or hotel doors.

Source: 14, 26

Built-up Tool Handles

For you who like to garden but find the usual tool handles too small to grasp firmly, try adding some bulk to the handle.

Use foam rubber to wrap around the handle until the size is comfortable for your hand. To secure the foam, wrap well with electrician's tape. This cushions your hand, adds bulk so the tool is easier to use, and it really works. This same technique can be used on other tools such as screwdriver or hammer.

197

Bowling Ball Guide

Would you like to bowl but don't have the strength to lift one of those heavy bowling balls? Here is an answer. A long-handled device for propelling and guiding a bowling ball down the alley can be purchased. You place the ball on the approach, or if you can't do that, have a friend do it for you. Place the aid behind the ball and push.

The handle is padded and the nylon tips that touch the sides of the ball help you aim for those pins. The handle is retractable for carrying.

Source: 29

Spiral-bound Books

Some of the paperback books published today are so tightly bound that it is difficult to keep them open to read. This problem is especially acute for those who have limited grasp or the use of only one hand.

You can have them rebound with a plastic spiral binding (like the one on this book). The book lies flat open and page turning is much simpler.

Most print shops can do this for you and the cost is nominal. They cut off the original binding, leaving all the printed material intact, and then add the spiral rings.

This is especially useful for some music books. Keeping them open on the piano or organ and using two hands to play is often impossible.

Playing Card Holders

It's fun to play cards—bridge, canasta, poker or cribbage—name your game. If you have the use of only one hand or a limited grasp, try one of these holders.

One rack is made of smoothly finished birch plywood and has four tiers to hold the cards. Cards are easy to see, to reach, and to play.

The other holder keeps the cards in a fan shape making them easy to see and to play. This eliminates the necessity of grasping the cards tightly during play.

Source: 16, 20, 23, 24

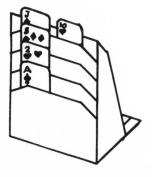

Playing Cards for Visually Impaired

All kinds of playing cards are available for people who have visual problems. The size is standard, which makes the cards easy to handle. The numbers and symbols are large.

Braille cards are also available for the blind. Some decks have both Braille and large numbers. These cards can be ordered for bridge or pinochle and the cost is comparable to that of regular decks.

Source: 2, 14, 20

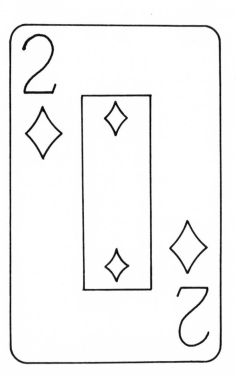

Drug Quackery

Have you been a victim of quackery? I hope not. Be aware of the ways that quacks prey upon their victims.

There are basically three types of quackery: false claims for drugs and cosmetics; food fads and food supplements; and fake medical devices. The object is not to restore your health, but to separate you from your money.

If your answer to any of these questions is "yes," you are likely being victimized.

1. Is the product or service a "secret remedy," available no other place?

2. Does the sponsor claim the medical profession does not accept his wonderful discovery?

3. Is the remedy being sold door to door or promoted by lectures from town to town?

4. Is this "miracle" drug, device, or diet being promoted in a sensational magazine, by a healer's group, or by some crusading organization?

5. Is the product or service good for a vast variety of illnesses, real or fancied?

If you think you are the victim of quackery, see your physician or inform your county medical society. If the product is promoted through the mail, inform the local Post Office.

Be alert! Help stamp out quackery!

Section 15

Publications and Health Groups

Recommended References

ACCESS TO THE WORLD

This book, published in 1977 by Chatham Square Press of New York City, offers all kinds of information about travel to the over 35 million physically handicapped people in the United States

Included are sections on air travel, buses, trains, ships, automobiles, hotels and motels, and many other travel tips. A section on health details information about food, water, immunizations, and finding medical assistance in a foreign country.

The author is Louise Weiss, an experienced traveler and author.

ACCENT ON LIVING

Accent on Living is a digest-size quarterly magazine with a wealth of helpful information for and about handicapped and disabled persons. To find out the current subscription price, write to Accent on Living, Inc., P.O. Box 700, Gillum Road and High Drive, Bloomington, Illinois 61701

IF YOU CAN'T STAND TO COOK BOOK

We who are ablebodied really have no idea of the many difficulties a person in a wheelchair experiences each day. For instance, the three times daily task of cooking can be next to impossible without physical changes in the kitchen area.

A creative author, who herself is handicapped, has written a cookbook entitled If You Can't Stand to Cook. This title has nothing to do with your desire to cook or the pleasure derived from cooking. She has collected more than 300 quick and easy recipes that can be prepared by a person in a wheelchair.

KICK THE HANDICAP: LEARN TO SKI

A handbook of information for the physically handicapped and others, compiled and edited by William E. Stieler. This handbook is sponsored by Adapted Sports Association, in association with other groups vitally interested and involved in teaching handicapped skiers. You can order this book from Kick the Handicap: Learn to Ski, Distribution Center, 6832 Marlette Road, Marlette, Michigan, 48453.

MEALTIME MANUAL

Mealtime Manual is prepared by the Institute of Rehabilitation Medicine, New York University Medical Center, in cooperation with Campbell Soup Company. It includes 250 pages of shortcuts, ideas, methods, appliances, and gadgets to ease your homemaking tasks (see source 20).

PRODUCTS FOR PEOPLE WITH VISION PROBLEMS

This catalogue is published annually with hundreds of items for the blind and visually impaired. This is a private, nonprofit organization. Their products are available at minimum cost and serve the needs of most people who have visual problems (see source 2).

REHABILITATION GAZETTE

A magazine published once a year for and by disabled persons is full of interesting information. *Rehabilitation Gazette* focuses on different subject matter in each issue and many back issues are also available. To inquire about current subscription price, write to Rehabilitation Gazette, Inc., 4502 Maryland Avenue, St. Louis, Missouri 63108

SELF-HELP MANUAL FOR ARTHRITIS PATIENTS

The manual, prepared by Judith Lannefield Klinger for the Allied Health Professions Section of the Arthritis Foundation, can be ordered from your local or state Arthritis Foundation. Many tools and devices are described and illustrated with a resource list in the back of the book. These same ideas are useful for persons with other ailments that curtail their strength and mobility. There is a charge for this manual (see source 4).

This large illustrated book offers many ideas to help the elderly and handicapped live more independently. Edited by Glorya Hale, published by Paddington Press, the book is available in both hard and soft covers. Six other contributors, two of whom are handicapped, have put together the most complete resource book you will find today.

Resources

Many of the items in this handbook can be purchased in your own home town—at the pharmacy, hardware store, fabric shop, lumber yard, "five and dime," or variety store. However, because many readers cannot browse and shop, wherever possible I have listed mail-order sources that will let you shop at home.

Most of the companies in this list publish catalogues. Some are free, but others require a small fee. Where a manufacturer is listed, please write to them and request the name and address of your nearest dealer.

Some of the devices pictured come in a variety of styles and not all of them are pictured. Prices vary from one outlet to another. You can "comparison shop" in your own home when you receive the catalogues of your choice.

Most of the products included have been tested and recommended by persons who have used them successfully. The author and publisher do not guarantee any of the products, but great care has been taken in their selection.

We hope you find this resource book helpful in your everyday living routine.

Resource List

1. American Cancer Society
   National Headquarters
   219 E. 42nd St.
   New York, New York 10017

2. American Foundation for the Blind
   Customer Service Department
   15 W. 16th St.
   New York, New York 10011

3. American Heart Association
   National Center
   7320 Greenville Ave.
   Dallas, Texas 75231

4. The Arthritis Foundation
   1212 Avenue of the Americas
   New York, New York 10036

5. B and B Lingerie Co., Inc.
   3527 Federal Way No. 78
   Boise, Idaho 83705

6. Eddie Bauer
   Third and Virginia
   Seattle, Washington 98124.

7. L. L. Bean, Inc.
   Freeport, Maine 04033

8. Bell Telephone Company
   (Your local office)

9. Cameo Stores
   Rockwell and Hartel Avenues
   Philadelphia, Pennsylvania 19111

10. Camp International, Inc.
    P.O. Box 89
    Jackson, Michigan 49204
    (Write for the nearest dealer outlet.)

11. Harriet Carter
    Department 82
    Plymouth Meeting, Pennsylvania 19462

12. Cemco
    P.O. Box 21
    Scandia, Minnesota 55073

13. Joan Cook
    P.O. Box 21628
    Ft. Lauderdale, Florida 33335

14. Walter Drake
    Drake Bldg.
    Colorado Springs, Colorado 80940

15. Fabric shops in your area or shops where sewing materials are sold

16. Fashion Able
    Rocky Hill, New Jersey 08553 (50¢)

17. The Ferry House
    554 N. State Rd.
    Briarcliff Manor, New York 10510

18. Foster House
    111 Foster Bldg.
    Peoria, Illinois 61632

19. Hardware stores in your area

20. Help Yourself Aids
    P.O. Box 192
    Hinsdale, Illinois 60521

21. Herrschner's Inc.
    Stevens Point, Wisconsin 54481

22. House of Minnel
    Deerpath Rd.
    Batavia, Illinois 60510

23. Independence Factory
    P.O. Box 597
    Middletown, Ohio 45042

24. Jar Opener
    P.O. Box 1644
    Ames, Iowa 50010
    (Send self-addressed stamped envelope for current price.)

25. Jodee Bra, Inc.
    200 Madison Ave.
    New York, New York 10016

26. Miles Kimball
    41 W. 8th Ave.
    Oshkosh, Wisconsin 54906

27. Left Handed Complements
    P.O. Box 647
    Brookline Village, Massachusetts 02147
    ($1.00 for catalogue)

28. J. C. Penney Catalogue
    (Available at any Penney store)

29. Pharmacies or hospital supply firms
    (Check your local directories.)

30. Plumbing shops
    (Check your local directories.)

31. Radio Shack (outlets in most major cities)
    Advertising Department
    1300 One Tandy Center
    Ft. Worth, Texas 76102

32. Ruthton Corp.
    2245 Pontius Ave.
    Los Angeles, California 90064

33. Sears Home Health Care Catalogue
    (Available at any Sears store)

34. Spencer Gifts, Inc.
    385 Spencer Bldg.
    Atlantic City, New Jersey 08411

35. Taylor Gifts
    355 E. Conestoga Rd.
    P.O. Box 206
    Wayne, Pennsylvania 19087

36. Variety or discount stores in your area

37. The Vermont Country Store
    Weston, Vermont 05161

212

38. Lillian Vernon
    510 S. Fulton Ave.
    Mt. Vernon, New York 10550

39. Vocational Guidance and Rehabilitation Services
    2239 E. 55th St.
    Cleveland, Ohio 44103 ($1.00)

40. Winfield Co., Inc.
    3062 46th Ave. N.E.
    St. Petersburg, Florida 33714
    (Write for the nearest dealer outlet.)

ASSOCIATIONS AND ORGANIZATIONS

American Association of Retired Persons
National Headquarters
1909 K St. N.W.
Washington, D.C. 20049

American Cancer Society, Inc.
National Office
777 3rd Ave.
New York, New York 10017

American Diabetes Association, Inc.
600 5th Ave.
New York, New York 10020

American Foundation for the Blind
15 W. 16th St.
New York, New York 10011

American Heart Association
National Center
7320 Greenville Ave.
Dallas, Texas 75231

American Medical Association
535 N. Dearborn St.
Chicago, Illinois 60610

American Occupational Therapy Association, Inc.
1383 Piccard Drive
Rockville, Maryland 20850

American Parkinson's Disease Association
147 E. 50th St.
New York, New York 10022

The Arthritis Foundation
1212 Avenue of the Americas
New York, New York 10036

Canadian Arthritis Society
77 Bloor St. West
Toronto, Ontario, M5 S2 V7

Federation of the Handicapped
211 W. 14th St.
New York, New York 10011

Institute of Rehabilitation Medicine
New York University Medical Center
400 E. 34th St.
New York, New York 10016

International Senior Citizens Association
11753 Wilshire Blvd.
Los Angeles, California 90025

Muscular Dystrophy Association of America, Inc.
810 7th Ave.
New York, New York 10019

National Association of the Physically Handicapped
2 Meetinghouse Rd.
Merrimack, New Hampshire 03054

National Congress of Organizations of the Physically Handicapped
7611 Oakland Ave.
Minneapolis, Minnesota 55423

National Council of Senior Citizens, Inc.
925 15th St. N.W.
Washington, D.C. 20005

National Council on Aging
1828 L St. N.W.
Washington, D.C. 21136

National Easter Seal Society for Crippled Children and Adults
2023 W. Ogden Ave.
Chicago, Illinois 60612

National Foundation—March of Dimes
Box 2000
White Plains, New York 10602

National Multiple Sclerosis Society
205 E. 42nd St.
New York, New York 10017

National Paraplegia Foundation
333 N. Michigan Ave.
Chicago, Illinois 60601

National Rehabilitation Association
633 S. Washington St.
Alexandria, Virginia 22314

National Safety Council
425 N. Michigan Ave.
Chicago, Illinois 60611

President's Committee on Employment of the Handicapped
Washington, D.C. 20210

Sister Kenny Institute
A/V Publications Office
Chicago Avenue at 27th St.
Minneapolis, Minnesota 55407

United Cerebral Palsy Association, Inc.
66 E. 34th St.
New York, New York 10016

INDEX

219